The Art of

Styling Sentences

20 patterns for success

by

MARIE L. WADDELL
Assistant Professor
Director of Freshmen English

ROBERT M. ESCH
Assistant Professor

ROBERTA R. WALKER
Assistant Professor

DEPARTMENT OF ENGLISH
The University of Texas at El Paso

BARRON'S EDUCATIONAL SERIES, INC.
Woodbury, N. Y.

Preface

The idea behind *20 Patterns* — the idea that students can learn to write by imitating patterns — grew out of our classroom experiences after we discovered that teaching by rules almost never will work, but that teaching by patterns nearly always will. Actually, this approach is not a new one. The teaching of writing by the imitation of patterns goes back to the pedagogy of the Renaissance; it was a common practice in the schools of Elizabethan England; it was certainly a widespread method of teaching in America from colonial times until early in the twentieth century. Our literary history shows that most great stylists of English — Shakespeare, Bacon, Donne, Milton, Jefferson, Churchill — learned to create good English sentences by imitating examples from earlier literary masters. Current novelists, popular essayists, and scholars in all fields, using as they do sentence patterns like the ones in chapter two of this book, also reflect in their writing their debt to the past, to the early masters of English prose.

The validity of teaching by imitation, by patterns for sentence structure and punctuation, became evident as we watched our students improve their ability to write, once they had sentences to imitate. Like Topsy, this book "just growed." It grew with help from colleagues in our department; our students helped us learn just what patterns they needed most often to get some style and variety in their writing; other teachers offered encouragement and many helpful suggestions as our patterns increased from ten to the present basic twenty. The book evolved still further as we presented these twenty patterns in an English journal, in a statewide meeting of college teachers, in numerous work-shops, seminars, and classes for graduate teaching assistants planning to teach English composition.

To our students who have mastered these patterns, who have made suggestions now reflected in the explanation sections, and who have contributed many of the examples, we are deeply grateful. We are deeply indebted to Dr. W. R. Lacey, Mrs. Piney Kiska, and Mrs. Marjorie

Cervenka who made valuable suggestions about the manuscript. We are also grateful to our other associates on this campus and elsewhere; their encouragement and support for this technique has helped us prove once again that the Renaissance tradition of teaching by imitation will work better than teaching by rules alone. We hope that this book will provide another link in that tradition.

Marie L. Waddell
Robert M. Esch
Roberta R. Walker

THE UNIVERSITY OF TEXAS
AT EL PASO
FEBRUARY 1, 1972

CONTENTS

CHAPTER 3

Sentences Grow Some More   76

CHAPTER 4

Figurative Language in Your Sentences   81

CHAPTER 5

The Twenty Patterns—In Print

Introduction

Almost anyone can benefit by learning more about writing sentences. You don't have to be a student in any school to benefit from this book; all you need is the desire to write well. And you must certainly want to create better sentences or you would not be reading this page. If you know how to write good, basic sentences yet find that they still lack something, that they sound immature because they have no variety, no style, then this little book is for you.

But if you want to write better sentences, how do you go about doing it? It's simple. You learn to write better sentences just the way you learn almost every other skill: by imitating the examples of those who already have that skill. You probably have already discovered that it is easier to master anything — whether it is jumping hurdles, doing a swan dive, playing the guitar, parking your car — if you are willing to practice imitating a model. Nowhere is this principle more obvious than in writing; just take Benjamin Franklin's word for it. If, like that shrewd man, you are willing to improve your writing skills by copying models of clear sentences, then this book with its five different chapters will help you to master the skill of writing anything well — even gracefully and with style.

CHAPTER 1 reviews briefly what constitutes a sentence. If you don't really understand the functions of different parts of a sentence, you may need a supplementary book with a fuller discussion of sentence structure. This chapter simply and briefly reviews the various parts of the sentence utilizing the traditional terms you will find in the explanations and descriptions of the patterns in Chapter II. Analyze these sentences until you understand their various parts.

THE WHOLE IS THE SUM OF ITS PARTS

CHAPTER 2, the heart of this book, contains twenty different sentence patterns, some with variations. If you study the graphic picture of each pattern (the material in the numbered boxes) and also notice the precise punctuation demanded by that pattern, you will then be able to imitate these different kinds of sentences in your own writing. The explanations under each boxed pattern will further clarify HOW and WHEN you should use a particular pattern; the examples following the explanations will give you models to study and to imitate. With these as guides, you should then practice writing and revising until you master the skill of constructing better sentences.

As you revise, take some of your original sentences and deliberately rewrite them to fit some of these patterns. This technique may at first seem too deliberate, too contrived an attempt at an artificial style. Some of the sentences you create may not even "sound like you." But what may seem like mere artifice at first will ultimately be the means to greater ease in writing with flair and style.

SKILL COMES FROM PRACTICE

Your first draft of any communication — letter, theme, report, written or oral speech — will almost always need revision. When you first try to express ideas in sentences, you are mainly interested in capturing your elusive thoughts, in making them concrete enough on a sheet of paper for you to think about them clearly. The second step in writing — in fact, where writing really begins — is revision. Indeed, as many great stylists agree and most students soon discover, good writing actually begins with rewriting. Since this is true, you must work deliberately to express your captured ideas in clear and graceful sentences.

CLEAR WRITING COMES FROM REWRITING

CHAPTER 3   will show you how some of the basic twenty styling patterns in CHAPTER 2 can combine with other patterns. Study the examples given and described in CHAPTER 3; then let your imagination direct your own efforts at making effective combinations of the different patterns.

COMBINATIONS LEAD TO ENDLESS VARIETY

CHAPTER 4   will show you how to express your thoughts in fresh, figurative language. Study the pattern for each figure of speech described there, and then deliberately try to insert an occasional one — simile, metaphor, analogy, or allusion — into your own writing. Try to be original; never merely echo or rehash some well-known, ready-made cliché. Create new images from your own experiences, from your own way of looking at life.

IMAGINATION IS ONE CORNERSTONE OF STYLE

CHAPTER 5 contains excerpts from the works of experienced writers who have incorporated patterns like these in their paragraphs. Study the marginal notes which give the pattern numbers you have learned from studying CHAPTER 2. Then go analyze something you are reading; discover for yourself how writers handle their sentences and their punctuation. And don't be afraid to imitate them when you write. You will, of course, find "patterns" (arrangements of words in sentences) which are not in CHAPTER 2 of this little book. Imitate others as well as the twenty we present.

UNDERSTANDING COMES FROM ANALYSIS

SUGGESTIONS TO THE INSTRUCTOR

Since this method of teaching students to write by imitation will be new to some instructors, we hope this section will offer suggestions that they will find helpful and practical. For the inexperienced teacher we want to anticipate some possible questions and provide some practical classroom guidelines; for the experienced teacher, we hope to offer a fresh approach to an old problem: getting students to write papers that are not too dull and boring for them to write or for the teacher to read. The following pages contain some hints for ways of teaching material in chapters one and two. Additional pages addressed to students will also suggest valuable ways for the teacher to present the patterns and other techniques to a class. (See pages xvi to xxii.)

Suggestions for teaching chapter one

As we said in the introduction to the book, CHAPTER 1 does not pretend to be a complete discussion of English sentence structure. The English prose sentence took several centuries to develop and is, as Sir Winston Churchill said, a "noble thing" indeed. There are entire books dedicated to an explanation of it; hence our coverage is minimal.

The main thing to do with CHAPTER 1 is to review with your class the five important "slots" in the standard sentence — subject, verb, complement, modifier, and connector. Be sure the students understand the terms and the functions of each. Give them some class practice in separating subjects from verbs in any of their current reading. It is sometimes easier for students to find the essential skeleton of the sentence if first they cross out, or put in parentheses, all of the prepositional phrases (which are usually mere modifiers, anyway). Then let them discuss the differences between phrases and clauses, between independent and dependent clauses, between declarative and imperative sentences. Never assume that your students will be very adept at this kind of analysis. They won't. Therefore guide them carefully with detailed explanation and many examples on the board.

Suggestions for teaching chapter two — the patterns

This chapter is the heart of *Styling Sentences* and contains enough material to keep your students busy throughout the semester as they incorporate it into their compositions. Pace your discussions to fit your class; don't go faster than your class can master the material, and never try to cover more than three patterns in any one class period. You will find that there is a kind of logic behind the grouping and arrangement of the patterns, so you might find it easier to go straight through from number one to number twenty instead of skipping around helter-skelter.

You are going to need to explain each of these patterns in great detail; you will also need to explain the rationale of the punctuation. Since one of the greatest teaching aids in the average classroom is the blackboard (yours may be green or blue!), don't hesitate to use it. Before you start with PATTERN 1, put some sentences on the board and review the sentence structure from CHAPTER 1. A good place to begin any kind of analysis of sentence structure is to have students put parenthesis marks around all prepositional phrases, using anything from their current reading — a textbook, the sports page, a wordy advertisement, lyrics of a popular song, or just the label on a ketchup bottle or a beer can! This is good exercise because prepositional phrases are nearly always modifiers of something and almost never a part of the basic sentence structure which just really has five "slots": subject, verb, complement, modifier, and connective.

Now, with your class, make up some graphic symbols to use when you analyze and discuss sentences or use something like the following:

1. Draw one line under the main clause (here, the entire sentence):

The atom bomb ‖ exploded man's old world and blew him into a new age.

2. Dramatize what happens when there are two independent clauses in the same sentence:

The atom bomb ‖ shattered man's old world (into smithereens;) it ‖ suddenly blew him (into a completely new kind) (of world).

Draw a dramatic circle between the two independent clauses (which *could* be separate sentences); then explain that only four things can happen here:

a. the period — which would separate these into two sentences;

b. a coordinating conjunction (*and, or, nor, for, so, yet*) preceded by a comma;

c. a semicolon — sometimes with an adverb like *therefore* or *however*;

d. a colon — but *only if* the second sentence explains or extends the idea of the first.

3. Use a bracket to set off dependent clauses and clarify their function as PART of the independent clause:

Marcie || bought [whatever she | wanted.]
[What Tatum | needs] || is more discipline.
The little Temple children || played [where the fallen leaves | were deep and soft.]

4. Use a wavy line under an absolute phrase:

The war being over at last, the task (of arranging the peace terms) || began.

5. Use a circle around connectors and other non-functional terms.

Next, it might be fun to show that these constructions work even with nonsense words. Do one or two and then let the class put their own creations on the board and explain them.

A brownsly swartian || swazzled (along the tentive clath.)
Yesterday I || thrombled (down the nat-fleuzed beach) [where glorphs and mizzles | lay (in the sun).]

After this review, your class should be ready to tackle the first group of sentence patterns — the compounds. All of them are really just two sentences in one, but with a vast difference that you must make clear. Now is the time to have the class really master the Checkpoints on page 15, the differences in the three compounds.

For exercises, you might consider these ideas

1. Follow up your discussion of particular patterns by asking students to write ten sentences of their own using the patterns you

assign. For easy checking have students label each sentence by putting the number of the pattern in the **left** margin. *The advantage of this book is the control you have through the pattern numbers.* For subject matter students can draw upon their reading background, hobbies, sports, other interests. If for any given assignment the entire class uses the same topic or idea, the sentences will be easier for you to check and more fun for the class to discuss, to compare how many different arrangements of words can express the same idea but with slightly different emphasis or rhythm.

2. Use SENTENCE PATTERN **1**, the compound with a semicolon and without a conjunction, to teach or to test vocabulary. In the first clause of the compound have students USE and UNDERSCORE the word in a sentence; in the second part have them DEFINE that word in a sentence.

> EXAMPLE: Zen Buddhism is an *esoteric* philosophy; only the initiated really understand it.

> OR THIS VARIATION

> The Greek root chrono means "time"; a chronometer measures time accurately. (See how much you can teach about punctuation in a sentence with this structure!)

3. Assign ten vocabulary words, each to be written in a different sentence pattern. Have students underscore the vocabulary word and label the pattern by number in the left margin. If students give the pattern number of the structure they are imitating, you can check the accuracy of their understanding of that pattern and its punctuation at the same time you are checking their vocabulary word.

4. Require students to have at least one different pattern in each paragraph of their compositions. For easy checking have them label each sentence by writing in the left margin the number of the pattern they are imitating. See "Marginalia" (pp. xviii-xxii) for more ways to encourage students in analyzing their writing as they improve their craftsmanship.

5. Have students collect interesting sentences from their reading

and make a booklet of fifteen or twenty new and different patterns with no more than two or three sentences plus analysis on each page. They may simply copy the sentences they find or they may clip and paste them to the booklet pages, leaving room for a description (analysis) of each sentence in their own words.

6. Take a long, involved sentence from the assigned reading; have your students rewrite it several times using four or five different sentence patterns. (These revisions may have to contain some words that the original does not have.) Have students read these sentences aloud in class, commenting on the various effects thus achieved.

7. Point out to students the effectiveness of incorporating SENTENCE PATTERN 8 (the one with two or three dependent clauses) in their thesis or using it to forecast their main points in the introduction or to summarize the entire composition in the conclusion.

8. Toward the end of the term, after they have mastered the patterns and know them by number, have students analyze some of their current reading, even from other courses. Have them write in the margin the numbers of the sentence patterns they find in other writers. (See CHAPTER 5 for two examples of this.)

TO THE STUDENT:

Suggestions for getting the most out of this book

The suggestions and exercises below may seem too simple or too artificial at first sight, but if you make a game of playing around with words, of fitting them to the formula, you will probably enjoy yourself. You will certainly learn how to write sentences that have some flair, and that is a skill worth developing because a well-constructed sentence is, like any artful design, the result of good craftsmanship; it actually involves and requires:

1. good composing or construction
2. accurate punctuation
3. a feeling for the rhythm of language
4. an understanding of idiom
5. clarity of expression.

If you are not in a composition class, but are working alone without a teacher's guidance, the suggestions below will help you to get the most out of this book, so do follow them carefully. Don't be afraid to copy a pattern and fit your own words into it. Remember that all great craftsmen begin as apprentices imitating a master. By following the suggestions below and mastering the sentence patterns, you will increase your skill in the art of styling sentences.

1. Study one pattern at a time. Write four or five sentences which follow that pattern exactly, especially the punctuation. Go through all twenty patterns in CHAPTER 2, taking only one at a time, until you are confident you understand the structure and the punctuation. Practice, practice — and more practice: this is the only way to learn.

2. In every paragraph that you write, try to incorporate one or more of these patterns, especially when you find yourself tending to write "primer sentences," those short and simple sentences having the same kind of subject — verb structure. Deliberately keep trying to improve the quality and arrangement of all of your sentences, whether they follow one of these patterns or not.

3. Think of something you want to say and then practice writing it in three or four different ways, noticing the changes in effect

and tone when you express the same idea with different patterns and punctuation. You may not be aware of these changes unless you read aloud, so do it often because reading out loud will train your ear.

4. Analyze your reading material for interesting sentences, ones that you think have good patterns which you could imitate. (CHAPTER 5 shows you how.) Whether you are reading a newspaper, a magazine article, or a skillfully styled literary work, you will find many sentences so well written that you will want to analyze and then imitate them. Underline them; learn the pattern. Or from your reading make a collection of sentences that you have especially enjoyed. Or keep a special notebook of new and different patterns that you want to copy. In short, look for new and different kinds of sentences in everything you read and make a conscious effort to add those new patterns to the basic twenty in CHAPTER 2.

Marginalia: To encourage deliberate craftsmanship

Analysis for Themes

In every theme or paper you write there should be some goals, some design that you are trying to fulfill. Marginalia can be a helpful guide for you, a way of checking up on what you are doing when you write. Marginalia is simply an analysis which you write in the left margin; it consists of words and symbols that indicate your analysis of what you do when you write.

In the first themes of the semester your teacher will probably be highly prescriptive, more than later on. When you are told how many words, how many paragraphs, sometimes even how many sentences should occur within paragraphs, don't resent the detailed directions. Think about them as training in a skill. After all, athletic coaches and music teachers alike begin their training with strict regulations and drills too. So follow all the "requirements." Eventually they will become a part of your skill as a writer and will become a regular, even automatic part of your writing. When they do, you can dispense with marginalia.

Things to do

1. Underline the topic sentence of each paragraph in colored ink, crayon, or pencil. Identify by the label T. S. in the margin.

2. In the **left** margin of each paragraph, other than the introductory or concluding paragraphs, mark one pattern from the SENTENCE PATTERNS. Mark in the margin SP #**6** or SP #**9a**.

3. Indicate a pronoun reference pattern in one of the paragraphs by drawing a circle around the pronouns and an arrow pointing to their antecedent. Identify in margin as PRO. PATT. or provide a legend at the bottom of your theme with all of the colors and their meaning.

4. Circle, in a different color, transitional words in one paragraph ("echo" words, transitional connectives, conjunctions).

5. List in the margin the types of sentences in one paragraph; be sure that there are simple (S), complex (CX), compound (C), and compound complex (CCX) sentences — at least one of each type.

6. When you master a new vocabulary word, underline it and label it VOC. in the LEFT margin.

You might use a different color for each type of entry; it would not only make the first and following drafts colorful, but would also let you see at a glance that you have incorporated all the devices and "gimmicks" of good construction. These marks might seem distracting at first, but the results will be worth the distraction. A mere glance at the marginalia will indicate whether you understand the composition techniques being taught.

Why bother with all of this? Because it works. There is no better answer. You will come to realize that themes must have a variety of sentences, that there must be transitional terms if the theme is to have coherence, that pronouns help eliminate needless repetition of the same word, that synonyms and figurative language give the theme more sparkle than you ever hoped for. Your teacher will like what he is reading; you will like what you are writing, and your marks will improve.

On the following pages are two paragraphs written by a freshman student. Notice his marginal analysis and the effectiveness of the different sentence patterns.

A paragraph analyzing a simile in poetry

THE MOVEMENT OF TIME

"Like as the waves make towards the pebbled shore,
So do our minutes hasten to their end . . . ."

—*William Shakespeare*, SONNET LX

T.S.

In the first two lines of Sonnet LX, Shakespeare uses a simile comparing the waves of the ocean to the minutes of our life: "Like as the waves make towards the pebbled shore, / So do our minutes hasten to their end . . . ." This line is inverted: that is, the subject — "our minutes" — is in the second line, and the comparison — "like as the waves" — is in the first line. The simile says, in effect, that "the minutes of our lives are like the waves on the shore." The waves roll endlessly, <u>inexorably</u> toward the shore of the ocean; the minutes of our lives hasten endlessly toward the end of our lives. This figure of speech gives an image of movement. We can almost see time, like ocean waves, moving toward its destiny: the end of life. Just as the waves end on the shore, so too our life's minutes end in death. Some words in the simile have particular power: the word *hasten* <u>conjures</u> up a mental picture of rapid movement, of inexorable hurry toward some predestined end. The word *towards* suggests a straight, unerring path going without hesitation or pause to some goal. The waves move toward their goal: the shore. Our minutes move toward their goal: life's end. This simile is a very effective, picture-making figure of speech. (It) paints a mental picture of movement and destiny. (It) suggests a very important (fact) about life, a fact we must remember. That (fact) is the truth expressed here beautifully by Shakespeare — life goes on forever toward its end, never slowing down or going back. Our lives do indeed "hasten to their end."

S.P. 3
S.P. 11

Voc.
S.P. 1

S.P. 10
S.P. 16
S.P. 3
Voc.
a repeated S.V.O. pattern

repeated S.P. 10

Pronoun pattern
S.P. 9

Repeat of key word

Summary of T.S. with "echo" of quote

A paragraph defining a word not in the dictionary

MARGINALIA

A JUNK-MAN

TS
Order: General
to Particular
SP4A

SP14
SP12

Voc.

Metaphor

Voc
SP1
SP10
and 4a

Contrast

SP9
Definition of T.S.

repeated word
for coh.
Example
factual data

Contrast
Voc. and two
levels of diction

A junk-man in baseball is the most feared pitcher of all. Most batters go to the plate with the knowledge that the pitcher usually throws either curves or fastballs or knuckleballs in the clinch. From his view at the plate, a batter sees a curveball pitcher's curve starting off in a line seemingly headed straight for his head. Fortunately, just before making any painful contact, the ball seems to change its own mind, veering away to the opposite side of the plate. But after long and arduous practice, any batter can learn to anticipate or recognize a curve and be prepared for it. The same is true for a fastball that blurs its way into the catcher's mitt or for a knuckleball which seems to have trouble deciding where to go. A veteran batter can learn to sense the sometimes erratic path of either ball; he can feel some confidence when he has some idea of the pitcher's preferred ball: a curve or a fastball or a knuckleball; he can even learn to make that wonderful contact which means a hit. But he can be put completely off stride when he hears he has to face that most dreaded of all pitchers, a junk-man — dreaded because he can throw all pitches with equal effectiveness and surprise. This element of surprise coupled with variety makes the junk-man the most feared of all pitchers in baseball. For example, when Sam the Slugger goes to bat, he can feel more relaxed if he knows that Carl the Curve-man will probably throw curves about seventy-five percent of the time; Sam can then, more than likely, be ready for at least one — which incidentally is all he needs to be ready for. The same is true for Sam when a well-known fastballer or knuckler is facing him from sixty feet away. On the contrary Sam the Slugger loses his equanimity and is tied in

SPI

"echo" of T.S.
for coh.

knots when Joe the Junk-man grins wickedly across that short sixty feet from mound to plate; Sam has no way to anticipate what surprises may lurk behind that wicked grin when he faces the most feared pitcher in baseball.

(The two paragraphs above are reprinted by permission of Shawn Waddell, *Freshman Composition* 3101, UTEP, Spring 1971, class of Roberta Walker.)

CHAPTER 1

THE SENTENCE

What exactly is a sentence?

Like sign language, the beat of drums, or smoke signals, sentences are a means of communicating ideas. They may express emotion, give orders, make statements, or ask questions; but in every case they are attempting communication.

In most sentences there are two parts which follow a basic pattern:

Subject || Verb

Occasionally, a sentence may be a single word. Who can argue that the following words, standing alone without modifiers, may sometimes communicate an idea?

What? Nonsense! Exaggerate.

In certain contexts "What?" and "Nonsense!" may communicate a complete thought. "Exaggerate," as you can see, has an implied "you" as its subject.

Now let's break up a very simple type of sentence into its two parts.

The bees are swarming.
The zebras stampeded.

bees || are swarming

Try making up your own example following the pattern above; box the subject and verb, and insert a pair of vertical lines between these two basic parts of the sentence. Only two slots are necessary — the S (subject) slot and the V (verb) slot.

Now let's add modifiers to the subject, to the verb, or to both. Note that you still have but two slots and need only one pair of vertical lines:

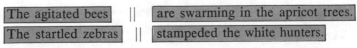

The agitated bees || are swarming in the apricot trees.
The startled zebras || stampeded the white hunters.

1

Combining the S slot and the V slot, you can construct the most common sentence pattern.

Each sentence pattern has a traditional name, describing its purpose and the task it performs:

TASK	NAME
A sentence may make a statement.	Declarative
May it also ask a question?	Interrogative
Let it give an order.	Imperative
What great emotion it can express!	Exclamatory

As you add words to modify the subject and verb, you will create longer sentences, some with phrases, others with clauses. Quite simply, a *phrase* is a group of words containing no subject—verb combination but acting as a modifier. Clauses, however, are considerably more complex. A *clause* is a group of words containing a subject—verb combination; sometimes the clause expresses a complete thought, but not always.

INDEPENDENT CLAUSE	makes a complete statement
	communicates an idea by itself
DEPENDENT CLAUSE	modifies a unit in another clause
	does not communicate a complete thought
	may be a unit in another clause.

These two types of clauses combine to form various types of sentences, but the most common sentences are these:

SIMPLE	makes a single statement
	is an independent clause
	has a subject and verb combination.
COMPOUND	makes two or more statements
	has two or more independent clauses
	has two or more subject–verb combinations.
COMPLEX	has an independent clause
	has one or more dependent clauses
	functioning as modifiers.

The subject—verb combination is the heart of each sentence you write. With this combination you can build an infinite variety of more complex sentence patterns. Each new subject—verb combination will require a new pair of ‖ lines. Longer sentences may have only one S and one V slot with one pair of vertical lines. Some times there will be only *one* S; sometimes there will be two or more subjects all in the same S slot because they come before the vertical lines separating S from V. The verb slot also may have one verb or several verbs.

<u>Cinderella</u> and <u>Frinella</u> ‖ <u><u>were</u></u> sisters but <u><u>hated</u></u> each other.

Sentences often have added attractions — something after the verb which is neither a modifying word nor a phrase, yet even these sentences may have but one S and one V slot. If the verb is transitive, you will find a direct object following it. In the following examples (all simple sentences), direct objects appear.

> EXAMPLE:　　<u>Benjy</u> ‖ <u><u>forgot</u></u> his galoshes.
>
> 　　　　　　<u>Agnes</u> ‖ <u><u>ignored</u></u> her teacher's glares and <u><u>continued</u></u> her mischief-making.

> NOTE:
>
> Throughout this chapter one line will underline the <u>subject</u>; two lines, the <u><u>verb</u></u>.

If the verb is intransitive, however, there may be subject completers (subject complements) which are nouns, pronouns, or adjectives. The following sentences illustrate the single S‖V combination with one or more subject complements.

> EXAMPLE:　　<u>Anne Boleyn</u> <u><u>was</u></u> Henry VIII's second wife.
>
> 　　　　　　Women's <u>emotions</u> <u><u>may be</u></u> ＿＿＿＿＿ or ＿＿＿＿＿, ＿＿＿＿＿ or ＿＿＿＿＿, ＿＿＿＿＿ or ＿＿＿＿＿.
>
> 　　　　(**YOU** *try filling in the blanks above!*)

To almost every part of the sentence you may add modifying words and phrases. You will still retain the single subject—verb combination or else expand your sentence to include several subject—verb combinations, all having modifiers. Distinguish main clauses by putting ‖

between the S V in the main clause and | between the S V in the dependent clauses; then underline independent clauses and put brackets around dependent clauses.

> EXAMPLE: *Long or short sentences || can sometimes communicate effectively the most difficult ideas in the world. (simple)*
>
> *Young women [whose skirts | were too short] and young men [whose hair | was too long] || marched around the Army recruiting station last month. (complex)*

Now let's break the whole sentence into its parts. When making a mechanical analysis of any sentence, you should use the following labels to identify the various parts:

S	subject	C	connective (conjunction)	M	modifier
V	verb	O	object of preposition	IO	indirect object
			object of infinitive		
SC	subject complement	P	preposition	DO	direct object

The following sentence illustrates the type of analysis you might practice:

M   M   M   S   V   M   SC   P M   O
The large floppy hat appeared unbelievably incongruous on the seamstress.

The following chapters in this manual will help you to write more effective sentences and will give you clues to spice up your dreary prose. As you will learn, sentences come to life as a writer plans them. Very few fine sentences are spontaneous. The following pages will show you models for sentences that you may imitate and utilize in your own writing. The patterns presented are basic ones, but by no means are they the only ones available to you. As your writing matures, you will discover additional patterns in your reading or even in your writing. As you master your ability to analyze and to compose sentences, you will justifiably be proud of your improving style.

And now you're off . . . on the way to creating better sentences, more polished paragraphs.

CHAPTER 2

THE TWENTY PATTERNS

Now let's make sentences grow . . .

In this chapter you will learn twenty basic patterns which writers frequently use to help give their style flavor and variety. These will not be new to you; you've already seen them many times in things you've read before. Perhaps you have never thought about analyzing them, never thought they could help you to perk up your prose. But they can.

Study them — give them a chance to help you.

Compound constructions

In the first chapter you studied the most elementary kinds of sentence patterns. The easiest way to expand the basic sentence pattern is simply to join two short complete statements (simple sentences) and thereby make a compound. When you do this, be sure to avoid the two pitfalls of the compound sentence:

1. the fused or run-on sentence (which has no punctuation between the two sentences you have now joined);

2. the comma splice (which is a mere comma instead of a period or semicolon or colon to separate the two sentences you have now joined).

A comma between independent clauses must have *and, but, or, nor,* or *for* with it. Of course, you will have no trouble avoiding these two problems if you faithfully copy the following patterns for compound sentences, being careful to copy punctuation exactly, too.

S____ V____ ; S____ V____ .

EXPLANATION:

This pattern helps you join two short, simple sentences having two closely related ideas. In other words, if *and* or *but* or *for* or *or* could join these statements, put them together in this compound pattern. Simply let a semicolon take the place of a conjunction with a comma. The graphic illustration in the box above and the examples below show only two clauses; you may, of course, have three or more.

And remember what makes a complete clause: a subject—verb combination which makes a full statement. In other words, an independent, complete clause must have some kind of verb; therefore look for one on each side of the semicolon. Remember that what precedes and what follows the semicolon in a compound sentence (PATTERN 1) must be capable of standing alone as a sentence all by itself.

THIS is a fragment:

The reason for the loss in yardage being the broken shoe-string on the left guard's shoe.

"Being" is not a verb; change it to "was" and make a sentence.

THIS is another kind of fragment:

Which was the only explanation that he could give at that moment.

This fragment is a dependent clause, in spite of the subject—verb combinations (*which was* and *he could*), because of the dependent word at the beginning. Remember this equation:

Because⎫
If   ⎬   +   a subject-verb   =   a fragment
When   ⎨   (plus) combination (equals) every time.
After   ⎭
and other such words

EXAMPLES:

Caesar, try on this toga; it seems to be your size.

Rage is anger beyond control; it is a joyful dictator of destruction.

The cry for freedom stops at no border; it echoes endlessly in the hearts of all men.

The vicuña is a gentle animal living in the central Andes; his fleece often becomes the fabric for expensive coats.

Despite its colorful blossoms the oleander is a dangerous shrub; the stems, when broken, exude a highly poisonous milky fluid.

Man is related to the monkey; only a monkey, however, would ever admit the relationship.

CHECKPOINTS:

✔ Check to see that on both sides of the semicolon there is a complete statement (sentence).

✔ After a semicolon there CANNOT be a construction like one of these:

    .... ;   which is the ....

    .... ;   the result being ....

    .... ;   although he never did ....

These three errors can be corrected with slight revision:

    .... ;   it is the ....,........

    .... ;   the result will be ....

    .... ;   he never did ....

✔ ALSO, the words before a semicolon must make a complete statement. Never put a semicolon after the following construction:

For example; ....

Because the snow was deep and the temperature below zero; ....

The work having been finished by five o'clock; ....

✔ These three errors can be corrected thus:
For example, ...
Because the snow was deep, the temperature fell below zero.
The work was finished by five o'clock.

✔ In short, don't confuse commas and semicolons.

In the space below, imitate this pattern and create some sentences of your own.

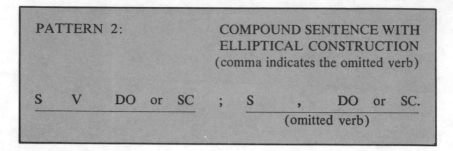

PATTERN 2:   COMPOUND SENTENCE WITH
              ELLIPTICAL CONSTRUCTION
              (comma indicates the omitted verb)

S   V   DO or SC   ;   S   ,   DO or SC.
                                (omitted verb)

EXPLANATION:

This pattern is really the same as PATTERN 1, but here you will omit the verb in the second clause BECAUSE and ONLY IF it would needlessly repeat the verb of the first clause anyway. In other words, the comma says to the reader, "Here you should mentally insert the same verb you have already read in the first clause."

This construction naturally implies a need for more or less parallel wording in both clauses; the verb, of course, must be exactly the same.

For example, this is not parallel:

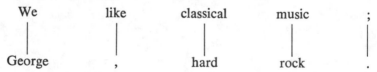

We   like   classical   music   ;

George   ,   hard   rock   .

The reader could not take the verb from the first clause and put it where the comma is, because "George like hard rock" is ungrammatical and improper. BUT even if your wording is parallel, even if the omitted verb is exactly like the one in the first clause, you may still have an awkward-sounding sentence if you forget the importance of rhythm and sound.

For example, read this aloud:

Darby played a musical number by Bach; Joan, Beethoven.

This sentence, read aloud, sounds as if Darby played something written by three people!

Then read this aloud:

> Darby played a musical number by Bach;
> Joan, one by Beethoven.

If you leave out more than the verb, you may need to insert some word like "one" here.

Notice in the sentence above and in the two below that it is possible to leave out more than just the verb itself; sometimes you may even leave out the subject *and* the verb:

> The feminine mystique is intuitive, not rational;
> aesthetic, not pragmatic.

> There's an interesting difference in books on the subject of sex:
> in handbooks about dating, the experts tell you how to avoid it; in handbooks about marriage, how to enjoy it.

EXAMPLES:

> The Eskimo lives in an igloo; the American Indian, in a teepee.
>
> The Scottish Highlander sports a tam-o'-shanter; the Texas Ranger, a Stetson or ten-gallon hat.
>
> Some note-takers try to take down all the information from the lecturer; others, only the main points.
>
> The Russian ballerina wears a tutu; the Malaysian dancer, a brightly colored sarong.
>
> The quest for righteousness is Oriental; the quest for knowledge, Occidental.
>
> A red light means stop; a green light, go.
>
> Terry always ordered a single dip of strawberry ice cream; Freddie, a banana split with pecans, two dips of chocolate fudge, and whipped cream on top.

CHECKPOINTS:

✔ Be sure that there really are two independent clauses here even though the second one has an unexpressed verb.

✔ Be absolutely sure that the verb omitted in the second clause matches exactly the verb in the first clause.

🖊 This rule applies to whatever you omit after the semicolon.

If you leave out more than the verb, be sure the structure is parallel and the thought is complete.

🖊 Use a semicolon if there is no conjunction; use a comma if there is a joining, coordinate conjunction.

In the space below, imitate this pattern and create some sentences of your own.

COMPOUND SENTENCE WITH EXPLANATORY STATEMENT
(clauses separated by a colon)

General statement (idea) : specific statement (example) .
(an independent clause)　　　(an independent clause)

EXPLANATION:

This pattern is exactly like PATTERNS 1 and 2 in structure: it is a compound; but it is very different in content, as the colon implies. A colon in a compound sentence performs a special function: it signals to the reader that something important or explanatory will follow (as this very sentence illustrates). In this particular pattern, the colon signals that the second clause will specifically explain or expand some idea expressed only vaguely in the first clause.

The first statement will contain a word or an idea that needs explaining; the second statement will give some specific information or example about that idea.

As you study the following examples, notice that the first independent statement mentions something in an un-specific way: "a harsh truth," "a horrifying meaning." Then the independent statement after the colon answers your questions: "What harsh truth?" "Which horrifying meaning?" In short, the second clause makes the first one clear.

EXAMPLES:

Darwin's *Origin of Species* forcibly states a harsh truth: only the fittest survive.

The empty coffin in the center of the crypt had a single horrifying meaning: Dracula had left his tomb to stalk the village streets in search of fresh blood.

Carry Amelia Nation and her female temperance league had a single goal: they hoped to smash every whiskey bottle and hatchet every saloon in America.

Pythons, anacondas, boa constrictors rely on the same technique to kill their enemies: they coil about their victims and crush them to death.

Creative writing is a little like biological creation: the offspring is sometimes quite different from the parent.

Young men should always follow this rule: always let her think she's getting her way even though you know better.

CHECKPOINTS:

✔ Now that you have learned all three of the compound sentences, notice the differences. PATTERNS 1, 2, and 3 are NOT simply three different ways to punctuate the same sentence. The words must perform different functions; the sentences must do different things.

PATTERN 1 must make two closely related statements about the same idea, statements you do not want to punctuate as two separate sentences;

PATTERN 2 must have the exact word or words from the first clause implied in the second — otherwise no ellipsis is possible;

PATTERN 3 must have a second independent clause that in some way amplifies or explains the idea stated in the first independent clause.

✔ You should not use this pattern with a colon unless the second statement is related to the first.

✔ Remember the test for all compound sentences: both clauses must be full statements and capable of standing alone as sentences.

In the space below, imitate this pattern and create some sentences of your own.

Sentences with series

What is a series?

A series is a group of three similar items, all of which go in the same slot of the sentence. All items in the series must be similar in form (all nouns or all verbs and so on) because they have the same grammatical function. You may have a series in any slot of the sentence: three or four verbs for the same subject; three or four objects for the same preposition; three or four adjectives or nouns in the object or complement slot. You may have a series with any part of speech, not only with single words but also with phrases or dependent clauses. You may have more than three items in a series, and you may also arrange them in different patterns:

A , B , C   A and B and C   A , B , and C

or with paired items: A and B , C and D , E and F

Remember to use commas between the items of all series.

When is a series helpful?

A series is a good way to eliminate wordiness. If, for example, you have three short sentences, reduce them to a single sentence with a series somewhere in it.

PATTERN 4:   A SERIES WITHOUT A CONJUNCTION
                  (a series in any part of the sentence)

A , B , C   .

EXPLANATION:

This pattern is the simplest form of the series. The items making up the series are separated by commas, and in this special pattern there is no conjunction linking the final two items. Omitting this conjunction in the series here is effective, for it gives your sentence a quick, staccato sound, a sound of crispness and liveliness.

Develop your ear!

Read the series aloud so you can hear whether the items flow together smoothly and euphoniously *without* the conjunction before the last item. Remember that tone and sound and fluency are important considerations here.

EXAMPLES:

The goals of the ecology-awareness movement are clear: breathable air, drinkable water, livable space, viable soil, an unpolluted ocean.

The wheat is packed into creaking wooden elevators, into bins of every description, into Quonset huts that scar the landscape — in fact into any available building.

The song swept through the world and told more to the people than all the books, all the speeches, all the pamphlets that had preceded it.

Shortly after midnight in a serene, enchanting, mysterious performance, the night-blooming cereus gradually begins to blossom.

With wisdom, patience, virtue, Queen Victoria directed the course of nineteenth-century England.

The United States has a government of the people, by the people, for the people.

CHECKPOINTS:

✔ Since any part of the sentence may have a series, you must take care to make all items in the series parallel in form as they are already parallel in function.

Find the items that are not parallel in this incorrect sentence:

Swimming, surfing, to go boating — these were Sally's favorite sports at the summer camp.

Now explain why this revision is better:

Swimming, surfing, boating — these were Sally's favorite sports at the summer camp.

NOTE: Although it is not a pattern discussed in this book, you may want to remember that the commonest pattern for series — A , B , and C — should always have the comma before the conjunction; otherwise, the reader may be confused or may completely misread the meaning:

Shakespeare uses an image, a metaphor, a simile and rhyme scheme to clarify his theme in this sonnet.

(A "simile and rhyme" scheme? Without the comma before the conjunction, that's what it says!)

The restaurant served four varieties of sandwiches: corned beef, pastrami, salami and egg with bacon.

(Would you order the last one?)

A or B or C
_____   .   (in any place in the sentence)
A and B and C
_____   .   (in any place in the sentence)

EXPLANATION:

Occasionally, you will want to vary the previous pattern and write instead a series with conjunctions between all items (but usually not for more than three). Again, let your ear be your guide.

EXAMPLES:

Peering down from the hill, Merlin could see the castle swathed in gloom and fear and death.

Despite his handicaps, I have never seen Larry angry or cross or depressed.

I would never react well to sudden blindness; I'd be weepy and depressed and resentful.

Once you master the rhumba and the tango, you can turn to the more difficult South American dances like the samba or the cha-cha or the mambo.

All that is good and decent and respectable seems abhorrent to some anarchists.

In the space below, imitate this pattern and create some sentences of your own.

A SERIES OF BALANCED PAIRS
(note the rhythm)

A and B , C and D , E and F .
(may be in any slot in the sentence)

EXPLANATION:

This pattern has a series with an *even* number of items — four or six or eight. Balance these in pairs with a conjunction between each of the items in the pair. This construction creates a balanced rhythm, but is this rhythm right for your sentence? Read the sentence aloud; listen to the rhythm of your words because *rhythm* is the important feature of this pattern. Does your sentence have an orderly progression with a kind of climactic order for the items? Can you hear the items balanced against each other? Do you like the way the paired words sound together?

(NOTE: There are other coordinating conjunctions besides *and* and *or*. See second example below.)

EXAMPLES:

Anthony and Cleopatra, Romeo and Juliet, Lancelot and Guinevere were all famous lovers in literature.

Eager yet fearful, confident but somewhat suspicious, little Johnny eyed the barber who would give him his first haircut.

Alexa could not decide whether humor or sorrow, gentleness or cruelty, hope or despair should be the hallmarks of her character.

His ambition and ruthlessness, his skill and cunning, his hatred and crimes helped to bring about the eventual downfall of King Richard III at the Battle of Bosworth Field.

Lorenzo had that paradoxical character of the Renaissance man
— idealist and materialist, artist and debauché, angel and
devil.

Jane Austen depicts with gentle satire the foibles and weaknesses,
eccentricities and ambitions, triumphs and defeats of the
human species.

AN INTRODUCTORY SERIES
OF APPOSITIVES
(with a dash and a summarizing subject)

Appositive , appositive , appositive — summary word S V.

(The key summarizing word before the subject may be one of these: *such, all, those, this, many, each, which, what, these, something, someone.* Sometimes this summary word will be the subject, but sometimes it will merely modify the subject.)

EXPLANATION:

This pattern begins with a "cluster" of appositives. An appositive is simply another word for something named elsewhere in the sentence — that is, it is another naming for some noun. After the appositives, there is a dash followed by a summarizing word and the subject—verb combination for the main clause. This word must sum up the appositives before it. These appositives you may arrange in any of the patterns for series (see PATTERNS 4, 4a, and 5).

A highly stylized sentence, this is an extremely effective pattern for special places in your writing, places where you want to squeeze a lot of information into the same slot.

EXAMPLES:

The trees and the earth and the green water on the lakes, the hills that were near and the far-off hills — all told their stories.

The crack of the lion trainer's whip, the dissonant music of the calliope, the neighs of Arabian stallions — these sounds mean "circus" to all children.

To struggle, to exist, and so to create his own soul — this is man's great task.

Love, hate, resentment, fear, anger, ambition — how many are the emotions that direct our day-dreams!

A. E. Housman, Lewis Carroll, Edward Fitzgerald — many in the nineteenth century achieved fame through their hobby, not their professional work.

The "Mona Lisa," *La Vita Nuova*, the frescoes in the Sistine Chapel — what an imagination those Italians had!

> **or:** — which of these is the best proof of the Italian imagination?

> **or:** — many are the wonders of the Renaissance in Italy.

An old photograph, a haunting fragrance, a sudden view of a half-forgotten scene — something unexpectedly triggers our nostalgia for the past.

NOTE: Sometimes these appositives can be at the end. Try reversing any of the sentences above, following the example of the sentence below:

The tea tax, the lack of representation, the distance from the Mother Country, the growing sense of being a new and independent country — what do you think caused the American Revolution?

What do you think caused the American Revolution — the tea tax, the lack of representation, the distance from the Mother Country, or the growing sense of being a new and independent country?

CHECKPOINTS:

✔ Check the punctuation of this pattern:

1. there must be commas between the appositives in the series;
2. there must be a dash after the series.

✔ Check to see that there is a summary word at the beginning of the main clause.

✔ As in any series, all these appositives must be parallel in structure and in meaning.

EXPLANATION:

The first of the sentence (or the last) is not the only place where you may have a series of appositives or modifiers. Appositives will re-name and modifiers will describe something named elsewhere in the sentence. Any kind of series (see Patterns 4, 4a, 5) may come between the subject—verb, between two subjects, somewhere in an inverted sentence (see Patterns 15 and 15a; also examples 2 and 3 below), and so on. Because this kind of series will be a dramatic interruption within the sentence and may even have commas, there *must* be a dash before and a dash after it.

EXAMPLES:

All the scholarly disciplines and especially all the sciences — physical, biological, social — share the burden of searching for truth.

"Which famous detectives — Sherlock Holmes or Nero Wolfe or Dick Tracy — will you take as your model?" the sergeant asked.

The necessary qualities for political life — guile, ruthlessness, and garrulity — he learned by carefully studying his father's life.

Young Beauregard — handsome, dashing, debonair, and full of élan — kept all the young ladies on southern verandas breathless, dreamy-eyed, yet despairing.

The American co-ed's dream — becoming a child bride, producing soggy babies, acquiring a suburban mortgage and a two-car garage — sometimes turns into a nightmare.

CHECKPOINTS:

✔ Do you have *two* dashes?

✔ It takes not one, but TWO, to make a pair.

✔ Can you read a "complete sentence" even after you eliminate the interrupting appositive or modifier? In other words, does the sentence convey its message without the words between the dashes? If so, you have punctuated properly, for the function of the dashes is to mark an interrupter that could be omitted.

A VARIATION:
A SINGLE APPOSITIVE
OR A PAIR

_____S_____ — appositive — _____V_____ .

(Use two commas or dashes or parentheses to enclose this appositive.)

EXPLANATION:

This pattern is like PATTERN 7 except that it has only one or two items for the appositive instead of a full series. Here, the appositive may be a single word or a pair of words; it may or may not have modifiers. In this variation, there is also an interruption in thought immediately after the subject, but here the appositive can have a variety of effects, depending on your punctuation:

a pair of dashes will make the appositive dramatic;

parentheses will make it almost whisper;

a pair of commas will make it almost inconspicuous becaus? they are so ordinary.

EXAMPLES:

A familiar smell — fresh blood — assailed his jungle-trained nostrils.

The ultimate polluter — you and I, my friend — must share the burden and the guilt for having created this dirty world.

Two phases in the creative process — discovery and invention — seem to reinforce each other.

His former wife (once a famous Philadelphia model) now owns a well-known boutique in the Bahamas.

The Elizabethan concept of artifice (craftmanship well-executed and therefore admirable) made the word "artificial" a compliment, not a criticism.

Her joyous shouts of laughter — a delight to all who knew her — no one will ever forget.

CHECKPOINTS:

✔ Again, it takes not one, but TWO, to make a pair — two dashes, two parentheses, two commas.

DEPENDENT CLAUSES IN
A PAIR OR IN A SERIES
(at beginning or end of sentence)

If . . . , if . . . , if . . . , then   S   V   .
When . . . , when . . . , when . . . , S   V   .
S   V   that . . . , that . . . , that . . . . .
(omit the third clause and have just two, if you wish)

EXPLANATION:

The preceding patterns have shown series with single words or phrases. This pattern shows a series with dependent clauses. All of the clauses in this series must be dependent; they must also be parallel in structure; they must express conditions or situations or provisions dependent upon the idea expressed in the main clause. This series of dependent clauses may come at the beginning or at the end of the sentence. You will normally have two or three clauses here; rarely will four or five sound graceful and smooth. Try not to struggle for style; be natural, relaxed, never forced.

This pattern is a very special one. Save it for special places, special functions. It is particularly helpful

1. at the end of a single paragraph to summarize the major points;
2. in structuring a thesis statement having three parts (or points);
3. in the introductory or concluding paragraphs to bring together the main points of a composition in a single sentence.

EXAMPLES:

Because it might seem difficult at first, because it may sound awkward or forced, because it often creates lengthy sentences where the thought "gets lost," this pattern seems forbidding to some writers, but it isn't all that hard; try it.

In Biology 3130 Stella learned that a hummingbird does not really hum, that a screech owl actually whistles, and that storks prefer to wade in water rather than fly around carrying tiny babies.

When he smelled the pungent odor of pine, when he heard the chatter of jays interrupting the silence, when he saw the startled doe, the hunter knew he had reached the center of the forest.

If you promise to keep your sox under the bed, if you agree to help me with the dishes every evening and take out the garbage pail every morning, if you really will "love, honor, and obey," then I might marry you.

Whether one needs fantasy or whether one needs stark realism, the theater can become a Mecca.

Since he had little imagination and since he had even less talent, he was unable to get the position.

CHECKPOINTS:

✔ Don't think there must always be three dependent clauses here. Two will work in this pattern also (see the last two examples above).

✔ Whether you have only two or a full series of three or more, whether you have the clauses at the beginning or end of the sentence, you should arrange them in some order of increasing impact (see fourth example).

Repetitions

What are repetitions?

A repetition is a restatement of a term; you may repeat the term once or several times within a sentence or a paragraph.

Why use repetitions?

Repetitions help to echo key words, to emphasize important ideas or main points, to unify sentences, or to develop coherence between sentences. Skillful repetitions of important words or phrases create "echoes" in the reader's mind: they emphasize and point out key ideas. Sometimes you will use these "echo words" in different sentences — even in different paragraphs — to help "hook" your ideas together.

How do you create repetitions?

Simply allow some important word to recur in a sentence or in a paragraph or even in different paragraphs. These "echo words" may come any place in the sentence: with the subjects or the verbs, with the objects or the complements, with prepositions or other parts of speech. You need not always repeat the exact form of the word; think of other forms the word may take, such as *freak* (noun), *freaking* (participle), *freaky* (adjective), *freakiness* (noun), *freakish* (adjective) *freakishly* and *freakily* (adverbs), and *freakishness* (noun).

Where are repetitions appropriate?

Repetitions are appropriate in two different places in the sentence:

1. the same word repeated in a different position in the same sentence (PATTERN 9);
2. the same word repeated in the *same* position (or "slot") of the sentence: for example, the same preposition repeated in a series or the same word used as object of different prepositions (PATTERN 9a).

How does punctuation affect the repetition?

Commas, dashes, periods, colons, and semicolons signal varying degrees of pause. A comma makes a brief pause, whereas a dash signals a longer pause. There is a kind of finality in the pauses created by the colon, the semicolon, and the period. The colon suggests that important words will follow, whereas the semicolon (like the period) is an arresting mark of punctuation signaling a full stop before another idea begins.

Consider these differences; decide what kind of pause you need; then punctuate, remembering that these marks are not really interchangeable. Each one suggests a different kind of pause.

NOTE: Once you have mastered repetitions in the same sentence, you will be ready to repeat some key words or phrases throughout your paragraphs, even from one paragraph to the next. In your reading, look for the many ways that writers effectively repeat some of their key words, scattering them around at various places in the sentence and in different places throughout the same paragraph. In one paragraph Rachel Carson, for example, used "sea" ten times; Winston Churchill repeated the phrase "we shall fight " eight times, using it to emphasize various points throughout one dramatic speech.

<u>S   V   key term</u>   —   . . . . .repeated key term   .

(use dash or comma before repetition)

EXPLANATION:

In this pattern you will repeat some key word in a modifying phrase attached to the main clause. You may repeat the word exactly as it is, or you may use another form of it: *brute* may become *brutal; freak* may become *freaky; battle* may become *battling*.

A key term is a word important enough to be repeated. It can come anywhere in the sentence, but the repetition of the word is most common toward the end. Or, if you have a key word in the subject slot of the sentence, the repetition of it may be, for example, a part of an interrupting modifier.

You may also vary this pattern slightly by using a dash instead of a comma; remember that the dash suggests a longer pause, a greater break in thought than the comma permits.

NOTE NUMBER ONE:

Be sure that the word is worthy of repetition. Notice how ineffective the following "little Lulu" sentence is, and all because of the repetition of an uninteresting, overworked word.

He was a good father, providing a good home for his good children.

NOTE NUMBER TWO:

Be sure that the attached phrase with the repeated key term is NOT a complete sentence; if it is, you will inadvertently create a comma splice, as here:

He was a cruel brute of a man, he was brutal to his family and even more brutal to his friends.

Here's one way of correcting the common splice:

> He was just a cruel brute of a man, brutal to his
> family and even more brutal to his friends.

EXAMPLES:

Every writer must obey what someone called the "eleventh commandment," the commandment not to puzzle his reader.

We all inhabit a mysterious, inorganic world — the inner world, the world of the mind.

A. E. Housman used this pattern #9 at the end of a famous lecture: "The tree of knowledge will remain forever, as it was in the beginning, a tree to be desired to make one wise."

In "The Lottery" Shirley Jackson mocks community worship of outworn customs, customs that no longer have meaning, customs that deny man his inherent dignity and link him with the uncivilized world of beasts.

Neither the warning in the tarot cards — an ominous warning about the dangers of air flight — nor the one on her ouija board could deter Marsha from volunteering for the first Mars shot.

Looking into the cottage we saw great splotches of blood smeared on the walls, walls that only that morning had rung with shouts of joy and merriment.

CHECKPOINTS:

✔ ✔ Double check! Notice that the repetition is in a phrase, not a clause. In this pattern, the words following the comma MUST NOT have a subject or a verb with the repeated word; the result would be a comma splice (comma fault).

WRONG: He was part of the older generation, his generation was born before the depression. (This compound must have a semicolon.)

CORRECT: He was part of the older generation, a generation born before the depression.

A common error occurs when there is a period or semicolon where the comma should be, thereby creating a fragment out of the modifier containing the repeated key term.

WRONG: He praises the beauty of his love. A love that is unfortunately hopeless because it is not mutual.

CORRECT: He praises the beauty of his love, a love unfortunately hopeless because it is not mutual.

NOTE: The first example contains the "pattern" of a very common fragment error:

$$\underline{\text{S} \quad \text{V} \quad . \quad \text{S} + \text{[dep. clause] but NO verb} \quad .}$$

In the space below, imitate this pattern and create some sentences of your own.

A VARIATION:
SAME WORD REPEATED IN
PARALLEL STRUCTURE

<u>S   V   repeated key word in same position of the sentence</u>   .

EXPLANATION:

Repetitions of words may occur in other ways, of course.

A. You may want to repeat some good adjective or adverb in phrases or clauses with parallel construction:

That South Pacific island is an *isolated* community, *isolated* from the values of the West, *isolated* from the spiritual heritage of the East.

B. You may repeat the same preposition in a series:

All revolutionists are negative; they are *against* things — *against* the values of the present and *against* the traditions of the past, *against* materialism and *against* mysticism, *against* taxation and representation and legislation.

C. You may repeat the same noun as the object of different prepositions:

This government is of the *people,* by the *people,* and for the *people.*

D. You may repeat the same modifying word in phrases that begin with different words:

Sidney devoted his life to those *selfish* people, for their *selfish* cause, but clearly with his own *selfish* motives dominating his every action.

E. You may repeat the same intensifiers:

Audrey appeared *very* chic, *very* soigné, *very* blasé.

Politicians concern themselves with *some* important issues, *some* burning questions, *some* controversy dear to their constituents.

EXAMPLES:

Few know my sorrow, fewer know my name.

"Porphyria's Lover" captures a moment of time, a moment of passion, a moment of tears.

His greatest discoveries, his greatest successes, his greatest influence upon the world's daily life came to Edison after repeated failure.

Taylor entered his sophomore year with renewed hope, renewed enthusiasm, renewed determination not to repeat the errors of his freshman year.

You must find other ambitions, other goals if your first ones don't work out.

**EMPHATIC APPOSITIVE
AT END, AFTER A COLON**

S   V   word: the appositive (the second naming)
                        (with or without modifiers)

EXPLANATION:

Often it is an idea, not a word, that you wish to repeat. Withholding it until the end builds the sentence to a climax and provides a pattern for a forceful, emphatic appositive at the end of the sentence where it practically shouts for your reader's attention. In the above pattern, the colon — because it is formal and usually comes before a rather long appositive — emphasizes this climax. Remember that the colon makes a full stop and therefore must come only after a complete statement; it tells the reader that important words or an explanation will follow.

EXAMPLES:

Most contemporary philosophies echo ideas from one man:
Plato, a student of Socrates and the teacher of Alexander.

A soldier goes AWOL for a very specific purpose: to hide from the MP's.

A teenage girl never forgets one thing: how to giggle.

Anyone left abandoned on a desert should avoid two dangers: cactus needles and rattlesnakes.

Were those twins my children, I'd make one thing clear to them: the curfew hour.

CHECKPOINTS:

✔ Check the words *before* the colon; be sure they make a full statement (sentence).

✔ After the colon, be sure to write only a word or a phrase — not a full statement (sentence). See PATTERN 3 above.

In the space below, imitate this pattern and create some sentences of your own.

A VARIATION:
APPOSITIVE (single or pair
or series) AFTER A DASH

S   V   word   —   the appositive
·   ·
(echoed idea or second naming)

EXPLANATION:

For variation, for a more informal construction, you may use a dash instead of the colon before a short, emphatic appositive at the end of a sentence. Notice that in both PATTERNS 10 and 10a, the second naming is usually climactic or emphatic. The difference is only in punctuation: dashes almost always precede a short, climactic appositive, whereas a colon will generally precede longer appositives.

Study the difference in sound and emphasis which punctuation and the length of the appositive make in the following sentences:

A new job requires one quality, humor.
    (common usage but not emphatic)   BLAH!
Adjusting to a new job requires one quality above all others —
    a sense of humor.   (dramatic signaling)
Adjusting to a new situation requires one quality: humor.
    (significant pause, but not so dramatic)
Adjusting to a new job requires one quality: the ability to laugh at
    oneself.   (more dramatic, more stylistically complete)

EXAMPLES:

Most contemporary philosophies echo ideas from one man —
    Plato.
The relatively few salmon that do make it to the spawning grounds
    have another old tradition to deal with — male supremacy.

The grasping of sea weeds reveals the most resourceful part of the sea horse — its prehensile tail.

But now there is an even more miserable machine tyrannizing man's daily life — the computer.

Skid-row inhabitants have one thing in common — a sense of defeat.

Oscar had only two ambitions — to marry a rich widow and retire to the Riviera.

CHECKPOINTS:

✔ The second naming must be a true appositive; don't simply "stick in" a dash or a colon before you get to the end of the sentence. If you do, you may have simply an error in punctuation, not a true appositive. Here is a poor example, lifted from a student's paper:

> One class of teenagers can be labeled — students.
>
> CORRECT: One label would fit almost any teenager: student.

In the space below, imitate this pattern and create some sentences of your own.

Modifiers

Adding modifiers is a good way to clarify a sentence that is too brief or lean. Often some key word will require additional explanation — modifiers — in order to make its meaning clear. Modifiers are especially helpful if you wish to appeal to your reader's senses, to add some figurative language, or to make comparisons or allusions.

These modifiers may be single words, phrases, even clauses; they may be at the beginning, in the middle, or at the end of the sentence. They may be ideas or descriptions or figures of speech which you add to a sentence you are revising. Take two short, ineffective sentences. Make one into a modifier or a dependent clause, and then combine it with the other sentence for a stronger, clearer construction.

You will have no trouble with modifiers if you remember one fact: like leeches or magnets, they cling to the nearest possible target. Therefore, take care to avoid misplaced or dangling modifiers. If they cling to the wrong target, you will have an incoherent or illogical or ludicrous sentence.

PATTERN 11:   INTERRUPTING MODIFIER BETWEEN S — V

S	,	modifier	,	V	.
S	—	modifier	—	V	.
S		(modifier that whispers)		V	.

EXPLANATION:

When the modifier comes *between* the subject and the verb, you may use a pair of commas or a pair of dashes to separate it from the main elements of the sentence. If the modifier is merely an aside within the sentence (a kind of whisper), put parentheses around it for variety in punctuation. This modifier need not be just a single word; it may be a pair of words or even a phrase.

EXAMPLES:

A small drop of ink, falling like dew upon a thought, can make millions think.

A small drop of ink, falling (as Byron said) like dew upon a thought, can make millions think.

His manner — pompous and overbearing to say the least — was scarcely to be tolerated.

NOTE: Interrupting modifiers may also come at some point other than between the subject and verb. See the following examples.

He jumped at the chance (too impetuously, really) to shoot the rapids in his kayak.

Her joyous bursts of laughter — delightful to all who knew her — no one will ever forget.

To be only a musician and nothing else — like an organ grinder or a gypsy fiddler — was an outrage Greg's family could not tolerate.

CHECKPOINTS:

✔ The punctuation marks for this pattern must go in pairs, with one mark before the modifier and a matching mark after it.

EXPLANATION:

The modifier that interrupts the main thought expressed by the subject—verb combination may be more than merely words or phrases. It may be a full sentence or even a full question or exclamation. If it is a full sentence, do not put a period before the second dash unless the sentence is a quotation. If it is a question or an exclamation, however, you will need punctuation. A question mark or an exclamation point may seem strange in the middle of a sentence, but this pattern requires such punctuation.

The interrupting modifier need not always come between the subject and verb; it may come in other places in the sentence (see the last two examples below). And notice the different signals that the punctuation gives the reader: parentheses really say that the material enclosed is simply an aside, not very important; the dashes, however, say that the interrupter is important to a full understanding of some word in the sentence.

EXAMPLES:

An important question about education — should universities teach the classics or just courses in science and practical subjects?— was the topic of a famous debate by Arnold and Huxley.

Narcissus ignored Echo so completely (how could he? she was such a lovely nymph!) that she just faded away.

Juliet's most famous question — early in the balcony scene she asks, "Wherefore art thou Romeo?" — is often misunderstood; she meant not "where" but "why."

One of Thoreau's most famous metaphors — "If a man does not keep pace with his companions, perhaps it is because he hears a different drummer. Let him step to the music which he hears, however measured or far away." — echoes Shakespeare's advice that each man should be true to himself.

Nelson made his tax report on New Year's Day — not with enjoyment (who could *ever* enjoy it?) — simply because he wanted an early return of his refund.

He jumped at the chance (too impetuously, I thought) to shoot the rapids in his kayak.

CHECKPOINT:

✔ Use this pattern with restraint. Otherwise your reader may think you have a "grasshopper mind" and never finish one thought without interference from another thought.

Participial phrase				
. . . .	,		S V	.

S V				
_____	,	Participial phrase		
		. . . .		.

EXPLANATION:

Modifiers come in a variety of forms — single words, groups of words, even clauses. One interesting kind of modifier is the participial modifier, a verb form that is a modifier instead of a verb. There are three types of participles:

> *present*   (ending in "ing")
>
> *past*   (normally ending in "ed")
>
> *irregular*   (so "irregular" that you will have to memorize these!)

> EXAMPLE: Persevering, determined to succeed, blest with discipline, the pioneers forged a civilization out of a wilderness.

> > *Persevering*   (present regular)
> >
> > *determined*   (past regular)
> >
> > *blest*   (past irregular)

The dictionary will help you with all participial forms. Remember that they all function as adjectives; that is, they modify nouns or words working as nouns.

Once you understand what a participle is, this pattern is simple. It shows participial modifiers at the beginning and at the end of the sentence, though of course they may also come as interrupters at any point in the sentence (see the first two examples under PATTERN 11).

50

CAUTION: Don't dangle participles! Give them something logical
to attach themselves to. You will have no trouble with
them if you remember not to "shift subjects" at the
comma: the idea or person you describe in the modifying phrase, not some other person or word, must be
the subject of your sentence. Inadvertent danglers sometimes result in unintentional humor or illogical statements:

Walking onto the stage, the spotlight followed the
singer.
Overgrown with moss, the gardener cleaned his seed
flats for spring planting.

See examples below for modifiers that don't dangle.

EXAMPLES:

Chaucer's monk is quite far removed from the ideal occupant of
a monastery, given as he was to such pleasures as hunting,
dressing in fine clothes, and eating like a gourmet. ("Given"
is the participle here.)

Overwhelmed by the tear gas, the rioters groped their way toward
the fountain to wash their eyes.

The wrangler reached for his lasso, knowing he must help to corral
the straying steers.

Printed in Old English and bound in real leather, the new edition
of *Beowulf* was too expensive for the family to buy.

Having once been burned on a hot stove, the cat refused to go
into the kitchen.

Modifier
. . . .   ,   S   V   .

(modifier may be in other positions)

EXPLANATION:

If you wish to place additional emphasis on any modifier, put it somewhere other than its normal place in the sentence. Sometimes in this new position the modifier seems so normal that it sounds clear without a comma; at other times, you *must* have a comma to keep the reader from misinterpreting your sentence. For example:

As a whole, people tend to be happy.
(Otherwise, "As a whole people . . . .")

To begin with, some ideas are difficult.
(To begin with some ideas?)

Sometimes a single word like "before," "inside," or "below" may look like a preposition instead of an adverb if you forget the comma in a sentence like this one:

Inside, the child   was   noisy.

Now look what internal rumblings you create when you have no comma:

Inside the child   was   noisy. (It *was?*)

If the modifier is clearly an adverb, however, you may not need the comma:

Later the child   was   quiet.

Using this pattern may help you to avoid another pitfall in writing sentences — the split infinitive. In the following sentence "occasionally" would be better at the beginning than where it is, separating the two parts of the infinitive.

Francesca liked to *occasionally wade*
in the neighbor's pool.

EXAMPLES:

Below, the traffic looked like a necklace of ants.

Frantically, the young mother called for help.

Frantic, the young mother rushed out the door with the baby in
her arms.

All afternoon the aficionados sweltered in the sunny bleachers
watching their latest idol from Mexico City.

The general demanded absolute obedience, instant and unques-
tioning.

Bert decided long ago to be a soldier of fortune.

The autumn leaves, burgundy red and fiery orange, showered down
like a cascade of butterflies.

A discussion argumentative yet inconclusive is likely to result when
two differing philosophies tangle.

In the space below, imitate this pattern and create some sentences of your own.

Inversions

Not all sentences need to start with the traditional subject—verb combination or with a modifier obviously meant for the subject. For variety you may wish to invert the normal order by beginning a sentence with some kind of modifier out of its normal place; even complements and direct objects may occasionally precede the subject. These modifiers, complements, and objects which you shift from their usual place may be single words, phrases, or dependent clauses.

Be wary of any inverted pattern, however. It might lead to awkwardness if your writing is undisciplined. Inverting the natural order should always result in a graceful sentence, not one that seems forced or like an intentional gimmick. Just as every sentence should seem natural, almost inevitable in its arrangement, so too must the one which departs from traditional sentence order. Try not to call attention deliberately to any inversion; make it fit into the context gracefully. Aim for sentences that possess the magic of variety, yes; but remember that too much variety, too obviously achieved, may be worse than none at all.

PREPOSITIONAL PHRASE
BEFORE S — V

Prepositional phrase   S   V   (or   V   S)
. . . .

EXPLANATION:

Before trying this pattern, remember what a preposition is. The very name indicates its function: it has a "*pre*-position." The "pre" means that it comes before the object which is necessary to make a prepositional phrase. In other words, a preposition never occurs alone because it must show the relationship between the word it modifies and its own object. For example, consider a box and a pencil. Where can you put the pencil in relation to the box? It might be "on the box" or "under the box," "in the box" or "near the box," "inside the box" or "beside the box." Can you think of other prepositions?

For this pattern, put the prepositional phrase at the beginning of the sentence, making sure that the inversion emphasizes the modifying phrase without sounding awkward. Only your ear will tell you whether to put a comma after it; will the reader need the punctuation for easy reading? If so, provide it.

For example, these sentences *must* have commas:

After that, time had no meaning for him.
Beyond this, man can probably never go.
(Not "after that time" or "beyond this man.")

These sentences do well without a comma:

Until next summer there will be no more swimming.
During the winter months Tom worked as a trapper.

EXAMPLES:

For every season of the year there is some magic, some unique delight.

Despite his Master's degree in World Trade and Economics, the only job Chester could get was making change in a Las Vegas casino.

With slow and stately cadence the honor guard entered the palace grounds.

Into the arena rushed the brave bulls to defy death and the matador.

In all the forest no creature stirred.

CHECKPOINTS:

✔ Sometimes a comma is necessary after the prepositional phrase, sometimes not. Let the sound and meaning of your sentence guide you.

OBJECT OR COMPLEMENT
BEFORE S — V

Object	or	Comp.	S	V	.

EXPLANATION:

Occasionally you may wish to invert and thereby stress some part of the sentence which ordinarily comes after the verb (the direct object or the subject complement). These may go at the beginning of the sentence instead of in their regular positions. This inversion adds invisible italics to the part of the sentence you write first. When you use this pattern, always read your inversion aloud to be sure that it sounds graceful in the context of your sentence, that it blends well with the other sentences around it. Here, as in the preceding PATTERN 14, only the sound and rhythm of the sentence will indicate whether you need a comma or not; there are no rules.

EXAMPLES:

These examples have the direct object before the subject—verb combination:

> His kind of sarcasm I do not like.

> Celia's interest in tarot cards and Sammy's absorption in horoscopes Mrs. de la Renza could never understand.

These examples have a subject complement before the subject—verb combination:

> An authority on Sanskrit, a dilettante, and an aesthete Geoffrey considered himself to be, but his friends had a different opinion.

> The Tin Lizzie may have been the most dependable automobile of its day, but quiet it wasn't.

CHECKPOINTS:

✔ Inversions are easy to do out of context, just for the exercise. But in a setting with your other sentences, you need to take care that they sound natural, not forced or awkward. Therefore use them sparingly, and then only for special emphasis.

OBJECT OR COMPLEMENT OR MODIFIER   V S   .

EXPLANATION:

The standard English syntax is

subject — verb

subject — verb — modifier

subject — verb — completer (direct object or subject
                                          complement).

Completely reversing the order of these sentence parts will
create an emphasis and a rhythm you can achieve in no other way:

verb — subject

modifier — verb — subject

completer — verb — subject.

This pattern will add spice to your prose; but like garlic or
cayenne pepper, too much can be overpowering. So restrain yourself; don't overuse this pattern. It will probably fit better into
dramatic statements or poetic prose passages than into business letters or laboratory reports.

EXAMPLES:

From the guru's prophecy radiated a faith that ultimately all would
be well.

Down the street and through the mist stumbled the unfamiliar
figure.

Even more significant have been the criticisms about the quality of
life in our affluent society.

Westward the country was free;   Mod S V C
westward, therefore, lay their hopes;   Mod V S

westward flew their dreams. It became for everyone the promised land of milk and honey.	Mod V S Prep. phrase out of place between V and S C

In "The English Mail Coach" DeQuincey has a sentence with PATTERNS 15 and 15a: "But craven he was not: sudden had been the call upon him and sudden was his answer to the call."

From his years of suffering came eventual understanding and compassion.

CHECKPOINTS:

✔ This pattern must never offend the ear by sounding awkward or stilted

✔ Test your sentence by reading it aloud. How does it sound?

✔ Is it consistent with your tone? Does it fit neatly into the context?

An Assortment of Patterns

PATTERN 16:				PAIRED CONSTRUCTIONS		
Not only	S	V	,	but also	S	V .
				(The *also* may be omitted.)		
Just as	S	V	,	so too	S	V .
				(may be *so also* or simply *so*)		
If not	S	V	,	at least	S	V .
The more	S	V	,	the more	S	V .
				(may be *the less*)		
The former	S	V	,	the latter	S	V .

EXPLANATION:

Some words work in pairs; for example, "either" takes an "or"; "not only" takes "but also." These correlative conjunctions link words, phrases, or clauses which are similar in construction. The patterns in the box above illustrate some common phrases used for paired constructions which may occur in simple or in compound sentences. You will find this structure particularly helpful in making a comparison or a contrast.

Whenever you use this pattern, remember to make both parts of the construction parallel; that is, make them both have the same grammatical structure and rhythm.

EXAMPLES:

Each man lives not only his personal life as a unique individual, but also the life of his contemporaries and of his epoch.

Just as wisdom cannot be purchased, so virtue cannot be legislated.

As things had begun, so they continued.

Reluctantly, every dieter looks for a favorable verdict from his bathroom scale: if not a pound less, at least not a pound more.

The more I eat chocolate fudge sundaes, the less I enjoy strawberry shortcake and other desserts.

Kai and Ernst were two of my favorite ski instructors: the former taught me downhill racing; the latter helped carry me to the hospital where Dr. Alexander set my fractured arm.

CHECKPOINTS:

✔ Remember that "pair" means "two." Be sure you have the second part of the construction; don't give the reader a signal suggesting two items and then provide only one. To say "Not only is she pretty" and then say no more is to leave your reader confused.

MORE PAIRS: The following list of correlative conjunctions might further aid you in developing this pattern:

whether . . . or	so . . . that
such . . . that	not only . . . more than that
both . . . and	as . . . as
neither . . . nor	not so . . . as

CAUTION: Put both conjunctions of the pair in a logical place so that what follows each one will be parallel.

WRONG: The prisoner was not only found guilty
of murder   but also   ↓ of robbery.
(no parallel verb here)

CORRECT: The prisoner was found guilty
not only of robbery
but also of murder.
(parallel construction;
better order for climax, too.)

WRONG: I not only forgot my keys
but also   ↓   my purse.
(no parallel verb)

CORRECT: I forgot not only my keys
but also my purse.

MORE PAIRED CONSTRUCTIONS, FOR CONTRAST ONLY

A "this, not that" construction

in some place other than the verb position

EXPLANATION:

This type of paired construction — the simple contrast — illustrates the differences between two ideas and usually involves a reversal. This simple contrast by reversal may be dramatically emphatic or may simply reenforce an ironic purpose. Unlike PATTERN 16, this one does *not* involve the correlative conjunctions. If you want to show a reversal in the middle of your statement, simply say something is "*this*, not *that*" or "not *this*, but *that*." Punctuation marks — especially commas, dashes, or parentheses — will help make a break in your sentence and establish your point of reversal or contrast.

EXAMPLES:

John could be a great dishwasher, but not a great chef.

She is a woman, but certainly no lady.

By just a quirk of fate (not by deliberate choice) Columbus landed in the Carribean, not the Gulf of Mexico; in the West Indies, not the East Indies.

Money — not love — was the reason the showgirl married the millionaire.

Blame Sara's poor manuscript on laziness, not fatigue.

We are not angry; simply disgusted and ready to quit.
(Note the ellipsis and the contrast.)

In the space below, imitate this pattern and create some sentences of your own.

DEPENDENT CLAUSES
(in a "sentence slot")
AS SUBJECT **OR** OBJECT
OR COMPLEMENT

S [dependent clause as subject]   V   .

S   V   [dependent clause as object or comp.]   .

EXPLANATION:

As you learn to vary your sentence structures, alternating simple ones and more complex ones, you will find this pattern especially helpful in achieving variety and style. Although this is a sophisticated pattern, it is (strangely enough) quite common in speech; it is easy to use in your written work, too, if you understand the dependent clause that is merely a part of the independent clause.

The dependent clauses in this pattern, which serve as nouns, will begin with one of the following words
who, whom, which, that, what, why, where, when
after which will come the subject—verb of the dependent clause. If one of these introductory words IS the subject, it will need only a verb after it.

EXAMPLES:

[*How he could fail*] is a mystery to me.
(subject of verb *is*)

He became [*what he had long aspired to be.*]
(complement after *became*)

[*What man cannot imagine,*] he cannot create.
(object of *can create* in this "inverted" sentence)

Juliet never realizes [*why her decision to drink the sleeping potion is irrational.*]
(object of verb *realizes*)

[*Why many highly literate people continue to watch insipid "situa-
     tion comedies" on television*] constantly amazes writers,
     producers, even directors.

(subject of *amazes*)

[*That he was a werewolf*] became obvious within a few moments
     after his fingernails turned into claws.

(subject of verb *became*)

CHECKPOINTS:

✔ Remember that the dependent clause can never stand alone;
it is only a portion of your sentence. Therefore don't put a period
before it or after it because you will create an awkward fragment.
For instance, these two examples are wrong:

With horror she realized that he was a werewolf. Con-
     firming her mother's low opinion of him.

Juliet never realizes why her decision to drink the sleep-
     ing potion is irrational. Which explains why she
     drinks it.

How would you correct these errors?

ABSOLUTE CONSTRUCTION
ANYWHERE IN SENTENCE
(noun plus participle)

Absolute construction   ,   <u>S</u>   <u>V</u>   .
· · · · · · · · · · · · · · ·

<u>S</u>   ,   absolute construction   ,   <u>V</u> .
(or a pair of dashes or parentheses)

EXPLANATION:

What exactly is an absolute construction? It is a noun or pronoun plus a participle with no grammatical connection to the independent clause. What's so absolute about it? Only its absolute independence, its lack of any grammatical connection to the sentence. At home in any part of the sentence, an absolute construction is a separate entity and provides further information without modifying anything. Maybe these constructions are called "absolute" because they are absolutely different from anything else in English grammar; they are not dependent clauses because they have no verbs, and they could never be independent clauses for the same reason.

ABSOLUTE: His blanket being torn, Linus cried on Charlie Brown's shoulder.

DEPENDENT CLAUSE: Because his blanket was torn, Linus cried on Charlie Brown's shoulder.

If carefully used, this pattern will be one of your most helpful devices for varying sentence structure. If tossed into a sentence cavalierly, it may create inexcusable awkwardness. Try not to force this construction but look for places in your paragraph where it would seem natural.

You may work with irregular participles (*torn* and *burnt* here):

His blanket torn and his finger burnt, Linus cried on Charlie Brown's shoulder.

Or you can work with present participles:

> The American economy, God willing, will soon return to
> normal.

> His early efforts failing, Teddy tried a new approach to the
> calculus problem.

If you wish, you may even use several participles and then contradict all of them with a contrasting adjective as the following sentence illustrates:

> Caesar continued his march through Gaul, his army tattered,
> exhausted, hardened — but victorious.

EXAMPLES:

> The walls being blank, the new tenant — an unemployed artist — promptly set about covering all of them in a mural of orange, vermillion, and yellow.

> I plan to sail to Tahiti (my pension permitting) as soon as I retire from this company.

> We had our Memorial Day picnic after all, the rain having stopped before sunset.

> The crayons being all used up, Angelo stopped marking on the newly painted table.

> All things considered, the situation seems favorable.

> My fortune having been told by Madame Lazonga, I felt more at ease about my future.

CHECKPOINTS:

✔ Because it has no grammatical connection with the sentence, the absolute construction must always have some punctuation. Use one comma after an absolute phrase at the first of the sentence or before one at the end. Such a phrase in the middle of the sentence must have a pair of commas or dashes or parentheses.

THE SHORT SIMPLE SENTENCE
FOR RELIEF OR
DRAMATIC EFFECT

<u>S   V</u>   .

EXPLANATION:

This pattern for a short sentence can provide intense clarity, but brevity alone will not make it dramatic. Actually, this pattern will be effective only

> when you employ it deliberately after several
> > long sentences,
> or when you let it more or less summarize what
> > you have just said,
> or when you let it provide transition between
> > two or more ideas.

"All was lost" or "Thus it ended" may not look very startling here, but in the appropriate context they might be quite dramatic. After a series of long, involved sentences, a statement with only a few words can arrest your reader's attention, make him pause, shock him into considering the ideas in the longer sentences that precede it. This pattern may, indeed, condense or point up what you have taken several longer sentences to explain.

Developing your style involves practice and training your ear to hear "a good turn of the phrase."

Polonius knew this.

EXAMPLES:

Days passed.
But then it happened.
All efforts failed.
Just consider this.

The frontier was open.

And so it was.

"Call me Ismael." (the dramatic first sentence in *Moby Dick*)

NOTE: Try to imagine the kind of context that would make these sentences dramatic and effective.

CHECKPOINTS:

✔ Length is not the criterion here.

✔ Don't think that "I like petunias" or "Children laugh" fit this pattern just because they are short. They might, of course, but only in the proper context.

✔ Look in your reading to discover how professional writers employ this technique of short sentences for special effects.

✔ This pattern is best when it is emphatic, points up a contrast, or summarizes dramatically.

| (Interrogative word) auxiliary verb | S | V | ? |

| (Interrogative word standing alone) | | | ? |

| (Question based solely on intonation) | | | ? |

| Auxiliary verb | S | V | ? |

EXPLANATION:

This pattern has two basic constructions: a question that begins with an interrogative word, or a statement that becomes a question through intonation (pitch or tone) of voice.

It is effective in several places:

in the introduction to arouse the reader's interest;

as a topic sentence to introduce a paragraph;

within the paragraph to provide variety;

between paragraphs to provide transition;

at the end to provide a thought-provoking conclusion.

Look in these five places to discover where a question could serve some desired effect in your writing. Provoke your reader with staccato-like questions, wake him up, make him pause and think, make him ask *why* or *wherefore* about your subject.

EXAMPLES:

What caused the change?
Then why did he?
What comes next?
When will it end?

These examples of questions made with intonation are more common in conversation than in formal prose:

That's her mother?
You made an A in Esch's class?
James flunked modern dance?

CHECKPOINTS:

✔ Questions need to be handled carefully to be effective.

✔ Avoid scattering them around willy-nilly just because they are easy; make them serve some purpose, such as to arouse curiosity, to stimulate interest, to lead the reader into some specific idea about your subject.

PATTERN 20: THE DELIBERATE FRAGMENT

Merely a part of a sentence .

EXPLANATION:

The mere mention of the word "fragment" chills the blood of grammar teachers; but a master stylist, ironically enough, often relies on brief sentence fragments to give emphasis and a sense of immediacy to his prose. This deliberate fragment should create a dramatic effect within your paragraph; it should serve some purpose. If it doesn't, don't use it. It would not be appropriate. Often only the context in which the fragment appears can tell you whether to put it in or leave it out. Used sparingly, the fragment can be as effective as the rhetorical question or the short dramatic sentence. Used injudiciously, it is simply another ineffective gimmick.

EXAMPLES:

Try a fragment
☆ in a description —

> I wish you could have known the Southwest in the early days. The way it really was. The way the land seemed to reach out forever. And those endless blue stretches of sky! The incredible clarity of air which made distance an illusion. I wish I could make you see it so you would understand my nostalgia, nostalgia and sorrow for a wonder that is no more.

☆ for transition —

> Now, on with the story.
> But to get back to the subject.
> So much for that.
> Next? The crucial question to be answered.

☆ in structuring a question or an answer —

> But how?
> What then? Nothing.

Based on logic? Hardly!

Where and when and why?

Upon what does wisdom finally depend? Primarily upon
the ability to know and understand — to see through
sham.

☆ for making exclamations and for emphasis —

What a price to pay!

All these achievements before his twenty-third birthday!

The next step — martyrdom.

There is a price to fame. The agonizing price of self-
denial, the price of blood and sweat and tears.

☆ and sometimes in aphorisms or fragments of clichés —

The more the merrier for them, too.

Early to bed!

A bird in the hand, old buddy. Remember?

Absolute power corrupting once more.

CHECKPOINTS:

✔ If you are in the habit of writing fragmentary sentences, don't
think that you have already mastered this pattern!

✔ Like PATTERNS 19 and 19a, this one must be a deliberate
styling device. It can never be merely an accident or a mistake in
sentence structure or punctuation.

CHAPTER 3

SENTENCES GROW SOME MORE

NOW you are ready to make sentences grow . . . and grow some more.

Now that you are familiar with some of the more complex patterns in CHAPTER 2, let's combine two or more of them to create additional variety in your sentences. Only a few examples of sentence combinations appear in this chapter, but you will discover many more possibilities as you experiment on your own, still remembering these cautions: always try to write a sentence which fits into the total context; never force a construction simply for the sake of variety.

Don't be afraid to be creative. Experiment not only with your own favorite patterns from CHAPTER 2 but also with others, with new ones you will discover in your reading or will create in your own writing by combining patterns as this chapter suggests. When you learn to maneuver sentence patterns, when you feel at ease manipulating words, then you will be a master of sentence structure if not yet a master stylist.

Now to discover what patterns combine well —

Combining the Patterns — Ten Ways

1. The compound sentence with a colon combines effectively with a series and the repetition of a key term (PATTERNS 3, 4, 9a)

    > To the Victorians much in life was sacred: marriage was sacred, women were sacred, society was sacred, the British empire was sacred.

2. Repetition also combines well with a dependent clause as the interrupting modifier (PATTERNS 9 and 11)

    > The experiences of the past — because they are experiences of the past — too seldom guide our actions today.

3. A dependent clause as complement combines well with an appositive at the end of a sentence after a colon and a series with balanced pairs (PATTERNS 17, 10, 5)

Ted became what he had long aspired to be: a master of magic and illusion, of hypnotism and sleight-of-hand tricks.

4. The series without a conjunction and the repetition of a key term combine well with the introductory appositive and an inversion of any kind (PATTERNS 4, 9, 9a, 15a)

The generation which was too young to remember a depression, too young to remember World War II, too young even to vote — from that generation came America's soldiers for Southeast Asia.

5. The compound sentence without a conjunction can combine with repetitions and series (PATTERNS 1, 4, 4a, 9)

Books of elegiac poetry had always stirred Jason; they made him think of music, music that sang of ancient glories, of brave men, of the things they loved and hated and died for.

6. Introductory appositives may be written as dependent clauses, with one of the clauses having a modifier out of place for emphasis, and the repetition of a key term followed by a question for dramatic effect (PATTERNS 6, 8, 9, 13, 19a)

That there are too many people, that overcrowding causes problems both social and economic and political, that human fellowship and compassion wear thin in such an environment — these are problems facing the inner city today, problems which eventually man must solve. But how will he ?

7. An inversion of the sentence pattern may also include a prepositional phrase before the subject—verb combination within a compound sentence (PATTERNS 1, 14, 15a)

Around Jay were men of various nationalities; with none of them could he ever really relate.

8. A pair of dependent clauses as direct objects will work well with paired words, a series without a conjunction, an interrupting modifier with dashes, and a repetition of the same word in a parallel construction (PATTERNS 4, 11, 9a, 16, 17)

The ambassador found that not only was America experiencing painful expansion and costly social upheavals — over foreign policy, racial disorder, economic priorities — but also that the nation was facing the threat of a national paralysis of will, a paralysis of faith.

9. An interrupting modifier that is itself a sentence may go well with another type of modifier (PATTERNS 11, 11a)

His family, a respected conservative family ruled mainly by several maiden aunts — his father had died when he was a child — had been scandalized at the thought that their young heir wanted to devote his entire life to hot-rod racing and roller-derby competition.

10. After a long involved compound sentence without a conjunction, a fragment with a repeated key word and then a fragmentary question may be very effective (PATTERNS 1, 4a, 9a, 20)

The ecology-awareness movement aims at balance and wholeness and health in our environment; it wants to assure a proper place in the scheme of things for people, for plants, and for animals. Not an exclusive place for either one, just a proper place for all. But how?

Expanding Sentences

Frequently writers find that a simple sentence with a single subject and a single verb is too brief or lean, that the meaning is not complete or as clear as it should be. What is missing is a modifier that will add explanations, descriptions, specific details, amplifications, supporting materials to make the sentence clear and meaningful to the reader. Thus, in order to make his point clear, the writer *adds* to his sentence. He uses modifiers to help the reader visualize; he illustrates the generalization expressed in his basic sentence. These modifiers may be words, phrases, clauses that appear at the beginning, the middle, or the end of the sentence; they may also modify one another.

Think of the basic idea, the primary simple sentence, as the first level of writing and the modifiers added for clarity as the second or the third or the fourth level of writing. Each successive level is related to the one immediately above it and is related to the basic sentence by the intervening modifiers, some subordinating, some coordinating. Later on, as you acquire more experience in writing, look for a generalization or an abstract word in your sentence — clear to you but possibly not to your reader — that will require you to shift down and backtrack, adding modifiers at different levels to help the reader comprehend fully the meaning you have in mind.

Study the examples below and notice how modifiers on different levels in the subject slot here help expand the sentence and clarify its meaning.

LEVEL ONE: the basic slots for any sentence   (S — V)
    Whooping cranes fly.

Now, on different levels add modifiers to the subject.

LEVEL TWO (the first modifiers):   may come before or after subject:

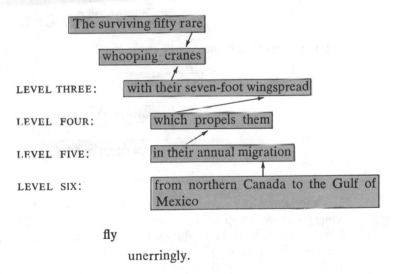

        fly
            unerringly.

Now add more modifiers on different levels in the verb slot:

LEVEL ONE　(the basic S—V):　Whooping cranes fly.

LEVEL TWO:　modifiers for the verb:

unerringly and swiftly overhead

LEVEL TWO EXPANDED (more modifiers for the verb):

as they migrate southward

LEVEL THREE:　modifier for some part of *that* modifier

using a kind of built-in radar

LEVEL FOUR:　more modifiers with more modifiers

in their search

for winter quarters

near Aransas Pass.

Now see what modifiers can do to a basic sentence:

The surviving fifty rare whooping cranes, with their seven-foot wingspread which propels them in their annual migration from northern Canada to the Gulf of Mexico, fly unerringly and swiftly overhead as they migrate southward using a kind of built-in radar in their search for winter quarters near Aransas Pass.

CHAPTER 4

FIGURATIVE LANGUAGE IN YOUR SENTENCES

Spice up your sentences with some interesting and original figures of speech. These are the fresh, poetic, picture-making phrases that say one thing but mean something different or something more.

Figurative language helps words say more and mean more than their actual, literal meanings convey. It demands something from the reader: he must understand the many connotations a word may have; he must see the picture or realize the image behind the figure of speech. It also demands something from the writer: he must try to avoid the colorless cliché. Once you understand what the various figures of speech are, once you master their "patterns," you will have no trouble thinking up original ones of your own.

SIMILE: A simile is a stated comparison between essentially unalike things, things from different classes. You must have one of the following connectives in all similes: *like, as, than,* or a verb such as *seems.* A simile says that two things are similar when they are not really alike at all.

EXAMPLES: Trying to pin a reason on the sudden elopement of those two is a little like trying to nail Jello to the wall.

It's about as easy as striking a match on a mirror.

Since 1945, the threat of total annihilation has roosted, like a vulture in a tree, in Western Man's awareness.

Betsy's first soufflé looked flatter than a punctured balloon.

The sky is like a blue tapestry.

Casanova found his mistresses's eyes were nothing like the sun. (This simile also makes an *allusion* to Shakespeare's Sonnet CXXX.)

METAPHOR: A metaphor is an implied comparison. It is implied because you do not say that something is "like" or "as" another thing; you simply say that one thing IS something else. (A is B.) As with similes, here again, the two things being compared must be unlike things from different classes.

There are really two kinds of metaphors.

1. The "A equals B" kind uses two terms.
   The sky is a blue tapestry.
   The dragonfly is a blue thread hovering over the pool.

2. The single-word metaphor can imply or suggest a comparison.

   a. *verbs*: Almost any sports page will yield a rich harvest of these verbs with picture-making power.

   The young rookie of the Milwaukee Bucks skyrocketed to fame.

   The quarterback blasted through the line of Nebraska's defense.

   The fans came unglued and jumped up in a frenzy of excitement.

   b. *nouns*: The image or picture of comparison comes implied in a noun which names one thing by calling it another; for example, see the word "harvest" in the sentence explaining *verbs* above.

The Arkansas defense line-up was a brick wall — impenetrable and invulnerable.

The quarterback crossed the line into the Promised Land, giving Ohio State six more points and a Rose Bowl win.

Harvard freshmen often think there should be an easier ascent up Parnassus than the one prescribed in the university catalogue.

c. *adjectives*: Adjectives may also imply comparisons; they describe something in terms that no reader would ever take literally.

Cynthia's feline movements clawed into Harold's composure. (Here, both "feline" and "clawed" are metaphors, suggesting something cat-like about Cynthia.)

"Every slaughtered syllable is a kindness to your reader," declared the lecturer addressing the budding young journalists.

CHECKPOINTS: ✔ Don't "mix" your images in a metaphor. Look at these ghastly creations!

They stepped forth into the sea of matrimony and found it a very rocky road.

The "ship of state" might be off its keel; it might sink or flounder or get off course without a firm hand at the helm, but it could never bog down in a storm of red tape or be the leader of the team or surge ahead in second gear.

ANALOGY: An analogy is really only an extended metaphor or simile. Analogy is an attempt to compare at length two objects from different classes; a classic analogy compares the human heart to a mechanical pump, for example, or the eye to a camera. This type of comparison carried to its extreme conclusion will, of course, be illogical because in no analogy will the various parts of the two unlike objects be completely comparable.

Analogy, however, does help you to clarify some comparison you are trying to make; if appropriate and not far-fetched, it will help you to sustain a clarifying comparison throughout a short paragraph or even a long, extended piece of prose. All analogies should help you to enrich your writing, to interpret some meaning or significance about your main points, to reflect your particular way of thinking about things, to add wit and charm to your style.

EXAMPLES: The New York Public Library might hold the key to your future; it unlocks many doors to knowledge; it opens the way to numerous opportunities.

(This would be merely metaphor unless you extended it a little further.)

The human brain in some ways resembles a computer.

(Now, go on — complete the analogy by showing how.)

Life is like the movies: there are many kinds of plots, but you should be the director of your own script.

(Does this suggest how you might discuss life as tragedy, comedy, melodrama, adventure?)

To the new student the college campus is like a forest — all trees, each indistinguishable from the other and each an obstacle in his path.

(Extend this analogy by describing how the student finds his way through the "forest" and comes to know the name — and function — of each "tree.")

CHECKPOINT: ✔ Never rely on an analogy as proof in logic or argument. An analogy is simply an imaginative comparison of two completely different things.

ALLUSION: Allusion is another way of making comparison; it suggests a similarity between what you are writing about and something that your reader has read before or heard about. The success of the allusion, of course, will depend on whether you strike a responsive chord in your reader's memory.

Allusions, richly connotative or symbolic, always suggest more than the words say. Because they are rich with overtones, your writing benefits by conjuring up for your reader all he remembers from his past reading or knowledge.

If you want to allude to something, let some word or phrase or even your very style refer to or suggest a similarity between the subject you are discussing and some other idea, a similarity real or imaginary. Success with allusions depends in part on your reader; after all, he must be able to recognize what you are alluding to. So choose allusions that will fit your audience as well as the context of your paper.

Remember that obscure allusions will cloud communication, but that good ones will enable you to say more in fewer words. Try to use fresh allusions in your sentences, for stale ones which have become clichés will merely bore your reader.

Common referents are history, the Bible, mythology, literature, popular personalities. In fact, a whole group

of words entered the language first as allusions to cele-
brities and entertainers: a political maverick, a boycott,
sandwiches, the Jack Benny walk, a Mae West suit, a
Morris chair. How many allusions can you find in popular advertising? Or in book titles? Or in popular music?

This Hallowed Ground (alludes to "The Gettysburg
Address")

Tender Is the Night (alludes to Keats' nightingale ode)

The Sun Also Rises (alludes to Ecclesiastes)

To Seek a Newer World (alludes to Tennyson's
"Ulysses")

Leave Her to Heaven (alludes to *Hamlet*)

These book titles have allusions; can you add other
titles to the list?

EXAMPLES: Even if you have miles to go, you should never abandon
a project without finishing it.
    (alludes to Robert Frost's "The Road Not
    Taken")

Deciding that a man's reach must exceed his grasp,
Charlie decided to continue trying for top billing
on the marquee.
    (alludes to Robert Browning's "Andrea del
    Sarto")

Flee now; pray later.   (In style, this should remind the
    reader of the familiar "Fly now;
    pay later" advertising slogan.)

The omnipresent ticking of the clock on the wall made
him feel chained to time.
    (alludes to Shelley's "Adonais")

Steve's roommate was the Cinderella man of big-time,
professional hockey.

CHAPTER 5

THE TWENTY PATTERNS— IN PRINT

TOUGH COUNTRY *
— from *Tularosa* by C. L. Sonnichsen

SENTENCE
PATTERNS

The Tularosa country is a parched desert where everything, from cactus to cowman, carries a weapon of some sort, and the only creatures who sleep with both eyes closed are dead. **11**

In all the sun-scorched and sand-blasted reaches of the Southwest there is no grimmer region. Only the fierce and the rugged can live here — prickly pear and mesquite; rattlesnake and tarantula. True, Texas cattlemen made the cow a native of the region seventy-five years ago, but she would have voted against the step if she had been asked. **14 10a 5**

From the beginning this lonesome valley has been a laboratory for developing endurance, a stern school specializing in just one subject: the Science of Doing Without. **14 10**

Everything has been done to promote the success of the experiments. There is almost no water; no shade. High mountain walls all around keep out the tenderfeet. On the west, screening off the Rio Grande valley with its green fields and busy highways, great ridges of limestone and granite — Franklin and Organ; San Andres and Oscuro — heave and roll northward from El Paso. Across the valley to the **9a 14 12 5 and 7 14**

eastward, shutting off the oases along the Pecos, the
Hueco mountains merge with the pine-cloaked Sacramentos, and these give way to Sierra Blanca and
Jicarilla, with 12,000-foot Sierra Blanca Peak soar-
ing in naked majesty over all.

12

The Tularosa country lies between the ranges,
a great pocket of sand, sun, and sparse vegetation
thirty miles wide, more or less, and over two hundred
miles long. The Jumanos Mesa, named for a long-
vanished tribe of Indians, gives it a northern boun-
dary. To the south it merges with the Chihuahua
Desert which pushes far down into Mexico.

11
11
14

Seen from the tops of the screening ranges, it
looks like a flat, gray-green, sun-flooded expanse of
nothing, impressive only because the eye can travel a
hundred miles and more in one leap. Near at hand
it is full of surprises. The northern end of the valley
is a little less parched. Grass still grows tall on Car-
rizozo Flat, and bean farmers have plowed up the
country around Claunch. Nearby, two prehistoric
lava flows cover the land with an appalling jumble of
volcanic rock known locally as the *malpais*.

12
4

13

South of the lava flows, the vast gypsum de-
posits called the White Sands spread out in a deathly,
glittering world of pure white which edges eastward
a few inches every year, threatening in a few millen-
nia to swallow up everything as far as the Sacramentos.

12

Sometimes the valley floor heaves in sand dunes;
sometimes it breaks into red hummocks, each one
crowned with the delicate green leaves and lethal
thorns of a mesquite bush. There are broad swales
where the yuccas grow in groves — leprous alkali
flats where even the sturdy greasewood can barely
hold its own — long inclines of tall grama grass
where the foothills rise to the knees of the mountains

1
9a 18

— and countless acres of prickly pear and *lech-uguilla* and rabbit brush.

4a

A harsh, forbidding country, appalling to newcomers from gentler regions. But it has its moments of intense beauty. Sunrise and sunset are magic times. Under a full moon, that lonely, whispering waste is transformed into an austere corner of fairyland. The belated traveler catches his breath when the tender fingers of dawn pick out the tiny black shapes of the pine trees far above him on the top of the Sacramentos. One does not forget the Organs blackening against the sunset, swathed in a veil of lilac shadows — the eerie gleam of the white sands at moonrise — a swarthy cloud dissolving in a column of rain, the froth of impact showing white at its foot while all round the sun shines serenely on.

20
19

14

12
4 (*with dashes*)
12
18

The yucca is a thorny and cantankerous object, but in the spring it puts up a ten-foot stalk which explodes in a mass of creamy-white blossoms. And so it is with other sullen citizens of the desert when their time comes: the prickly pear with its rich yellow flower, the desert willow dripping with pendent pink and lavender, little pincushion cacti robing themselves in mauve petals more gorgeous than roses, the ocotillo shrouding its savage spines in tiny green leaves till its snaky arms look like wands of green fur, each one tipped with a long finger of pure scarlet.

10

4

18

It is big country — clean country — and if it has no tenderness, it has strength and a sort of magnificence.

9
16a

To live there has always been a risky business — a matter not only of long chances and short shrifts but also of privation and danger. This was true of the prehistoric cave dwellers who lived only a little better than their animal neighbors in the Huecos many centuries gone by. It was true of the little

16 and 5
(*note repetition of "true" in parallel construction here*)

pueblo communities which grew up later in the mountain canyons and wherever a wet-weather lake made existence possible on the valley floor. It was true in historic times of the peaceful Christian Indians who abandoned their unfinished church at Gran Quivira when the Apaches overwhelmed them nearly three hundred years ago.

Yes, it has always been hard country — frontier country — and for obvious reasons, the first reason being those same Apaches. The slopes of the Sierra Blanca were their favorite haunts as far back as we have any records, and though they ranged far and wide over the desert and even moved to Mexico for decades when the Comanches descended upon them, they always came back to the mountain rivers and the tall pines. A merciless environment made them tough and almost unbeatable fighters. They kept their country to themselves as long as they were able, waging a never-ending war against hunger and thirst, Comanches and Mexicans, soldiers and settlers, until their power was broken less than a lifetime ago.

Highways and railroads were slow in coming to a region so far removed from the gathering places of men and money. Sheer isolation did what the Apache was not able to do alone: it held off the traders and developers for years while the Rio Grande and Pecos settlements were booming.

But the most potent force of all for keeping people out was plain, old-fashioned, skin-cracking drought. The rainfall was imperceptible, and there was just enough ground water available to cause trouble. On the valley floor there was next to none at all until men got around to drilling wells. A few springs existed here and there in the Organs and the San Andres, none of them big enough to supply more than a few men and beasts. The eastern mountains

9
9 and 18

12 and 5

17
3

4

14

were higher and better supplied. Spring-fed streams
came down from the Sierra Blanca at Three Rivers,
while Tularosa Creek descended the pass between
Sierra Blanca and Sacramento beside the main trail
from the Pecos to the Rio Grande.

Farther south, where the mile-high cliffs of the   13
Sacramentos soar above the plain, a number of canyons drained off the water from the heights — Dog   10a
Canyon and Agua Chiquita; Sacramento and Grape-   5
vine. In Sacramento Canyon and in Dog Canyon the   14
water was more or less permanent. But everywhere,
until the skill and cupidity of man turned the liquid   19
gold to account, it flowed out onto the flats a pitifully
short distance and disappeared in the sand. Along
with it, as the years passed, flowed the blood of   15a
many a man who gave up his life for a trickle of
water.

Sensible men, cautious men, stayed away from   9a
such a place. But the adventurous and the hardy   4a
and the reckless kept on coming. Each one had a
dream of some sort — water for his cows, solitude   4
for his soul, gold to make him rich. For even the
Tularosa country has its treasures. The ghostly ruins
of Gran Quivira have been honeycombed by men
obsessed with the notion that the Indians buried a
hoard of gold before they left. At the northeast   14
corner of the valley, in the Jicarilla Mountains, lies
the abandoned gold camp of White Oaks, the site   15a
of rich mining properties seventy years ago. Midway
between El Paso and Alamogordo, on the rocky
slopes of the Jarillas, Orogrande sits solitary, remem-   12
bering the days when prospectors and miners
swarmed in; and a few miles away at the San
Augustin Pass the abandoned shafts at Organ tell
a similar tale.

But the real story of Tularosa is the story of

Texas cattlemen — drifting herdsmen who began
to invade the valley in the early eighties, bringing
their stern folkways with them. They too ran into
trouble, for their law was not the law of the Mexicans
or the Indians or the Yankees who arrived during
and after the Civil War. It was those proud riders
who kept the Old West alive in that lonely land until
yesterday. It was the clash of their ways and standards with the ways and standards of the settled
citizens which caused the feuds and killings and
hatreds that make up the unwritten history of the
region. The Apaches and the climate and the lay of
the land helped. But in the last analysis it was the
Texans who made Tularosa the Last of the Frontier
West.

10a
12

4a
*note parallel
"it was"
construction*

9
4a

4a

Those times seem as remote from present-day
reality as the wars of Caesar and Charlemagne, but
they have left a brand on the soul of many a man
and woman still living. That is why this story has
never been fully told — why all of it can never be
told. For out here in the desert the West of the old
days has never quite given way to a newer America.
Customs have changed, but attitudes have held fast.
To test this fact, try asking questions about certain
people and events. Old men clam up and change the
subject. Young ones who have heard something
hesitate a long time before telling what they know
about the sins and tribulations of their grandfathers.
Once it was dangerous to talk about these things.
Even now it is not considered wise. The fears and
loyalties and customs of yesterday — these things
still cast their shadows on us who live on the edge
of the desert. On the streets of El Paso or Las Cruces
or Alamogordo you can still hear the click of boot-
heels belonging to men who played their parts in
dramas which would make a Hollywood movie look

17
9a

19
19
6

14 and 4a

tame. Their sons and daughters still live among us —
fine people, too — and their friends still frown on   7a
loose discussion.

For these reasons this is not an easy story to   14
tell, but it is time someone told it. So let's go back
to the beginning, before the Texas cattle crowded in,
ate the grass down to the roots, and trampled the
plain into dust — back to the days when the country   9
was the way God made it: bunch grass growing up
to a horse's belly; miles of yellow flowers in the wet
years; little rainwater lakes at the foot of the Organs   4
and the San Andres, long since dried out and buried   12
in dust; sun and sand and sixty long miles to town.   4a

EXCERPT FROM A *THOUSAND DAYS* *

Arthur M. Schlesinger, Jr.

SENTENCE
PATTERNS

After Kennedy's death, Adlai Stevenson called him the "contemporary man." His youth, his vitality, his profound modernity — these were final elements in his power and potentiality as he stood on the brink of the Presidency. For Kennedy was not only the first President to be born in the twentieth century. More than that, he was the first representative in the White House of a distinctive generation, the generation which was born during the First World War, came of age during the depression, fought in the Second World War and began its public career in the atomic age.

14
4 and 9a
6

9

This was the first generation to grow up as the age of American innocence was coming to an end. To have been born nearly a decade earlier, like Lyndon Johnson, or nearly two decades earlier, like Adlai Stevenson, was to be rooted in another and simpler America. Scott Fitzgerald had written that his contemporaries grew up "to find all Gods dead, all wars fought, all faiths in man shaken." But the generation which came back from the Second World War found that gods, wars, and faiths in man had, after all, survived if in queer and somber ways. The realities of the twentieth century which had shocked their fathers now wove the fabric of their own lives. Instead of reveling in being a lost generation, they set out in one mood or another to find, if not themselves, a still point in the turning world. The predicament was even worse for the generation which had been too young to fight the war, too young to recall the age of innocence, the generation which had experienced nothing but turbulence. So in the fifties some sought security at the expense of identity and became organization men. Others sought identity

11
11

9a
4

14

9a
9

note parallel cst.

at the expense of security and became beatniks. Each   19
course created only a partial man. There was need
for a way of life, a way of autonomy, between past   9
and present, the organization man and the anarchist,   5
the square and the beat.

It was autonomy which this humane and self-
sufficient man seemed to embody. Kennedy simply
could not be reduced to the usual complex of socio-
logical generalizations. He was Irish, Catholic, New
England, Harvard, Navy, Palm Beach, Democrat
and so on; but no classification contained him. He
had wrought an individuality which carried him be-   5
yond the definitions of class and race, region and   16
religion. He was a free man, not just in the sense of
the cold-war cliché, but in the sense that he was,
as much as man can be, self-determined and not the
servant of forces outside him.

This sense of wholeness and freedom gave him
an extraordinary appeal not only to his own genera-
tion but even more to those who came after, the   16
children of turbulence. Recent history had washed
away the easy consolations and the old formulas.
Only a few things remained on which contemporary
man could rely, and most were part of himself —   10a
family, friendship, courage, reason, jokes, power,   4
patriotism. Kennedy demonstrated the possibility of
the new self-reliance. As he had liberated himself   16
from the past, so he had liberated himself from the
need to rebel against the past. He could insist on   4 (verbatim
standards, admire physical courage, attend his church,   series)
love his father while disagreeing with him, love his
country without self-doubt or self-consciousness. Yet,
while absorbing so much of the traditional code, his
sensibility was acutely contemporaneous. He voiced
the disquietude of the postwar generation — the   10a
mistrust of rhetoric, the disdain for pomposity, the
impatience with the postures and pieties of other days,   4

the resignation to disappointment. And he also voiced
the new generation's longings — for fulfillment in
experience, for the subordination of selfish impulses
to higher ideals, for a link between past and future,
for adventure and valor and honor. What was for-
bidden were poses, histrionics, the heart on the
sleeve and the tongue on the cliché. What was re-
quired was a tough, nonchalant acceptance of the
harsh present and an open mind toward the unknown
future.

4a

*parallel cst.
with pattern*
17

This was Kennedy, with his deflationary war-
time understatement (when asked how he became a
hero, he said, "It was involuntary. They sank my
boat"); his contempt for demagoguery (once during
the campaign, after Kennedy had disappointed a
Texas crowd by his New England restraint, Bill Att-
wood suggested that next time he wave his arms in
the air like other politicians; Kennedy shook his head
and wrote — he was saving his voice — "I always
swore one thing I'd never do is — " and drew a picture of a man waving his arms in the air); his freedom from dogma, his appetite for responsibility, his
instinct for novelty, his awareness and irony and
control; his imperturbable sureness in his own pow-
ers, not because he considered himself infallible, but
because, given the fallibility of all men, he supposed
he could do the job as well as anyone else; his love
of America and pride in its traditions and ideals.

19

1

*4
and
4a*

16

* Reprinted by permission of Houghton Mifflin Company.
©1965 by Arthur M. Schelesinger, Jr., *A Thousand Days*,
pp. 113-115.

Suggested Review Questions

1 & 3

1. Explain the difference between the compound sentence with a semicolon and one with a colon. What is the specific difference in the second clause?

2. What kind of verb must be "understood" in the second clause before you can omit it?

2

Can you ever omit something other than the verb in an elliptical construction?

4 — 8

3. What kinds of things can be listed in series? What slots in the sentence contain series?

Explain the patterns and the punctuation for the different kinds of series.

4. In PATTERN 6, what two things come immediately after your series of appositives?

5. Why must the series in PATTERN 7 be set off by a pair of dashes?

What other marks of punctuation might occasionally substitute for those dashes?

6. In what two particular places in an essay would PATTERN 8 be good to use? What should go into the dependent clause?

7. What other patterns could perform the same function?

9

8. What qualifications should a word have before you put it in PATTERN 9?

9. What kinds of words and in what slots of the sentence can you repeat the same word in parallel structure?

9a

10. What kind of construction must come after the comma to keep PATTERN 9 from becoming a PATTERN 1 with a comma splice?

9

PATTERN
NUMBERS

10 & 10a

11. Write one sentence three times, using different punctuation marks before the appositive (comma, dash, colon). Then explain the difference in emphasis which the punctuation creates. Which is least emphatic? Which is most emphatic?

Which makes a longer pause? Which is most formal and prim?

12. What besides a single word can be an appositive?

13. *a.* What is the difference in the construction following the colon in PATTERN 3 and PATTERN 10?

    b. What is the difference in the construction following the dash in PATTERNS 9 and 10a?

7a & 11

14. Explain the difference between an internal appositive and an interrupting modifier.

11

15. In PATTERN 11, what two main parts of the sentence are separated by this interrupting modifier?

11

16. What three marks of punctuation can separate this modifier from the rest of the sentence? Can you ever use just ONE of these marks?

17. Write the same sentence three times. Punctuate it with a pair of commas, a pair of dashes, and a pair of parentheses; then explain the difference in sound and emphasis in each.

11a

18. Write a sentence that functions as an interrupting modifier in another sentence.

11a

19. Write a question as an interrupting modifier. Where does the question mark go?

12

20. Where do participles come from? How are they always used? What different kinds of endings may they have?

PATTERN NUMBERS		
12	**21.**	How can you avoid a dangling participle here?
13	**22.**	What kind of modifier needs a comma after it in PATTERN 13?
14	**24.**	What purpose might lead you to invert a sentence?
15	**23.**	What does "inverted sentence" mean?
15	**25.**	What items in the normal order of a sentence may come out of their normal place (i.e., be inverted)?
15a	**26.**	What cautions must you observe to make your inversions successful?
16	**27.**	What kind of phrases (words) always come in pairs?
16	**28.**	What kind of statement will this pattern help you to make?
17	**29.**	What kind of "signal words" herald the beginning of dependent clauses that may function as subject or object or complement?
	30.	Write two sentences using the same dependent clause. In one sentence, make the dependent clause the subject; in another, make it the direct object.
18	**31.**	Describe an absolute construction; name its two parts. Can it ever be a complete sentence?
18	**32.**	What is the difference in this pattern and the one with an introductory or concluding modifier?
18	**33.**	If the absolute construction occurs in the middle of the sentence, what must your punctuation be?
18	**34.**	Can absolute constructions ever occur in pairs or in series?
19	**35.**	What is the difference in PATTERN 19 and the ordinary kind of short simple sentence?

PATTERN NUMBERS	
19	**36.** What special functions can this pattern perform?
19	**37.** Why is the sound of this pattern so important? the rhythm? the context?
19a	**38.** What special functions can the short question perform?
19a	**39.** What are the two types of questions?
19a	**40.** Where are good places to use a short question in writing?
20	**41.** What two reasons may make a writer use a deliberate fragment?
20	**42.** What is the importance of the surrounding context for a deliberate fragment?
20	**43.** What different kinds of functions may the fragment perform?

MISCELLANEOUS QUESTIONS (for class discussion or essay tests)

44. Write the same sentence twice and punctuate it two different ways. Discuss the difference in sound, emphasis, and effect.

45. Write a sentence with S – V – D.O. Now put that D.O. in a different place and notice the effect.

46. Express the same idea with different kinds of phrasing:

Bad grades bother John.

What bothers John is bad grades.

John is bothered by bad grades.

John, bothered by bad grades, decided to buy some midnight oil.

Bad grades bothering John?

Bad grades having bothered him before, John determined that this semester would be different.

PATTERN
NUMBERS

47. Make up some sentences with nonsense words and discuss the structure and punctuation involved.

48. Define certain terms which occur in CHAPTER 2: *elliptical, appositive, parallel construction, participle, absolute construction, series, modifier.*

49. What function does punctuation play in most sentences?

50. Why are style and variety in your sentence structure so important anyway?

Why Punctuate?

Long association with the printed page has made most readers expect certain signals to conform to standard conventions.

denrael evah lla dluoc eW

sdrawkcab sdrow daer ot

tes dah sretnirp ylrae fi

yaw taht epyt rieht

upside-down is really no trick at all.

and most people find that reading

Also, we know the shapes of printed words so well that

we can read almost anything when only the tops of letters show

but we have more difficulty when we can see only the bottoms.

The same kind of training has made us come to expect that printed words today will have spaces between them even though in many early writings allthewordsrantogetherwithoutspacesanywherenotevenbetween sentencesandtherewerenosuchthingsasparagraphs.

In the same way, we have come to expect that punctuation will follow conventions just as we expect to read from left to right and to find spaces between words so do we also expect the marks of punctuation to signal to us something about the relationships of words to each other after all the same arrangement of words for example Joe said Henry is a dirty slob can have two different meanings depending on the punctuation even a few marks to signal the end of each sentence would have helped you in this paragraph to help your reader give him some of the conventional signals we call punctuation marks.

Punctuation: A Signal System

In the American English sentence, punctuation functions as a code, a set of signal systems for the reader to which he will respond. If your code is clear, the reader will get your signals. If your code is faulty, the reader

---

Format for this page was partly suggested by John Spradley's article—"The Agenwit of Inpoint"—in JETT (*Journal of English Teaching Techniques*), Spring, 1971, pages 23-31.

will be confused and you will have failed to communicate. Some marks guide the eye; others, the ear. That is, they indicate the intonation (pause, stress, pitch) the reader should use mentally. For instance, the period indicates a full stop with pitch of voice dropped to indicate a long pause, whereas exclamation points "shout" at the reader and indicate he must raise his voice. The period indicates a long pause, whereas the comma indicates a short one. The semicolon signals not only a stop but also "equality": something equally structured will follow. The colon signals that the thought is not complete, that something explanatory will follow: an important word, phrase, sentence, or a formal listing. The colon is a very formal mark, whereas the dash is less formal, and material within parentheses just "whispers" to the reader. Generally speaking, these marks are not interchangeable; each mark has its own function to perform. It is important, therefore, that you learn when to use the following punctuation marks:

COLON:

1. to introduce enumerations after a complete statement

2. before an independent clause which restates in different form the idea of the preceding independent clause (in a compound sentence)

3. to indicate something is to follow, after the words "following," "as follows," or "thus"

4. before a climactic appositive at end of sentence

SEMICOLON:

1. between the independent clauses in a compound sentence without a conjunction

2. between the independent clauses in a compound sentence with a conjunction when there are commas in one or both clauses

3. before transitional connectives (conjunctive adverbs) separating two independent clauses (*however, therefore, furthermore, thus, hence, likewise, moreover, nonetheless, nevertheless*)

4. to separate elements in a series containing internal commas

COMMAS: to separate main sentence elements

1.   independent clauses joined by coordinate conjunctions (*and, but, for, or, nor, so, yet*)

2.   elements in a series

3.   contrasted elements in a *this, not that* construction

4.   direct quotation from such constructions as *He said, She answered*, etc.

5.   elements in dates, addresses, place names

6.   long introductory phrase or an adverbial clause preceding the main clause

7.   an inverted element

8.   any elements that might be misread or which might otherwise seem to run together

9.   important omissions, elliptical constructions

10.   absolute constructions at the beginning or the end of a sentence

COMMAS: a pair to enclose

1.   any interrupting construction between subject and verb, verb and object or complement, or any two elements not normally separated

2.   an appositive

3.   nouns or pronouns of direct address

4.   non-restrictive (*not* essential) interrupting modifiers

5.   absolute constructions within sentences

6.   any parenthetical expression within sentences

DASH: to separate sentence elements

1.   before a summary word to separate an introductory series of appositives from the independent clause

2.   before an emphatic appositive at the end of a sentence

3.   occasionally before a repetition for emphasis

DASHES: a pair to enclose

1.   an internal series

2.   abrupt changes in thought or pronounced sentence interrupters

3.   parenthetical elements, often for emphasis

4.   interrupting modifiers and appositives for dramatic effect

PARENTHESES

1.   to enclose words, phrases, or expressions that have no bearing upon the main idea (to make asides or "whispers" to the reader)

> NOTE: Like commas and dashes, parentheses may occasionally be used also:

2.   to enclose an interrupting series

3.   to enclose an appositive

4.   to enclose an interrupting modifier between subject — verb

PERIOD

1.   at the end of a declarative sentence

2.   after abbreviations

QUESTION MARK

1.   at the end of a direct question

2.   after each question in a series
     Where are the jewels? the crown? the rings? the tiaras?

3.   in parentheses to express uncertainty
     In 1340 (?) Chaucer was born.

> NOTE: Don't use a question mark to indicate
>
> a.   *intended irony*:   His humorous letter failed to amuse her.
>
> b.   *an indirect question.* Joe asked when we were going to have chiles rellenos again.

  c. *courteous requests*: Will you please pass the
           the butter.

EXCLAMATION POINT

1. at the end of sentences with strong exclamations or commands, those that show strong emotion
2. after strong interjections

QUOTATION MARKS

1. periods and commas ALWAYS GO INSIDE QUOTATION MARKS!
2. colons and semicolons ALWAYS GO OUTSIDE QUOTATION MARKS!
3. question marks and exclamation points go inside or outside depending upon the context of the sentence
4. enclose the actual words of a speaker
5. identify symbols, letters, words used as such (He has too many "but's" in this paragraph, and his "$" sign is a simple "S.")
6. enclose the titles of short stories, poems, paintings, songs, essays, chapters of books, BUT NOT book titles